The
CROMFORD
CANAL

The
CROMFORD
CANAL

HUGH POTTER

The
History
Press

Frontispiece: Two boats are sunk in the foreground of this delightful study of Leawood Pump House and its reflection, probably in the late 1960s. An old ice-breaker lies rotting where it was abandoned by the last maintenance staff on the canal. Beyond it is a small work punt. In the 1980s, after the canal had been drained for maintenance work and refilled, the ice-breaker floated and was towed to Cromford Wharf, where attempts to pull it out of the water broke its back. Since then it has gradually rotted away and, in 2003, only the metalwork remained. (Johnny Walker)

First published in 2003 by Tempus Publishing
Reprinted 2006

Reprinted in 2009 by
The History Press
The Mill, Brimscombe Port,
Stroud, Gloucestershire, GL5 2QG
www.thehistorypress.co.uk

British Library Cataloguing in Publication Data.
A catalogue record for this book is available from the British Library.

ISBN 978 0 7524 2802 4

Typesetting and origination by
Tempus Publishing Limited.
Printed in Great Britain.

Contents

This warehouse stood at the end of Stone Row in Golden Valley, until the early 1900s. It had more than one use over the years, as can be seen from the two rows of infilled windows. At some time it was thought to have been used as living accommodation, and possibly a church. Standing on the wharf to the right is Israel Hawkins, who delivered coal locally for the Butterley Company. The boat is a 'spoon dredger', the operation of which is described on page 111. Note the winch on the front to draw the boat forward. (Doris Ball)

Acknowledgments

Thanks are due to the many people who have generously given their time or loaned photographs. Initials in brackets indicate photographs from the collections of the following: the late Ike Argent (IA); Mick and Carole Golds (MG); Heanor & District Historical Society (HD); Brian Key (BK); Laurence Knighton (LK); Brian Lamb (BL: ©Brian Lamb collection DN36 5AJ); Ian Moss (IM); John Pass (JP); Frank Rodgers (FR); Simon Stoker (SS); Len Waller (LW) and Robin Witter (RW). The Waterways Trust has provided images as follows: British Waterways Archive (TWT/B); B.W. Archive, Arthur Watts Collection (TWT/W); Boat Museum, Robert Aickman Collection (TWT/A); Boat Museum, Michael Ware Collection (TWT/M).

Thanks also to Ann and Marianne at High Peak Junction and the Derbyshire County Council Rangers, especially Andy, Bob and Robin.

In addition to those supplying photographs and information, thanks are also due to Euan Corrie, Mike Harrison, Brian Key, Val Roberts and Liz Tatam for checking the layout and text. Any errors, however, are mine!

Opposite below: Wigwell or Aqueduct Cottage is perhaps the most recorded feature on the canal, from the early days of photography up to the present day. It was originally built by Peter Nightingale for the controller of the lock at the entrance to the Leawood Arm, adjacent to Wigwell or Leawood Aqueduct. Sadly, the once pristine cottage, seen here at the beginning of the twentieth century, has been uninhabited for some fifty years and is now little more than a ruin. The bridge in the foreground has, however, been rebuilt. (Ivy Turberville).

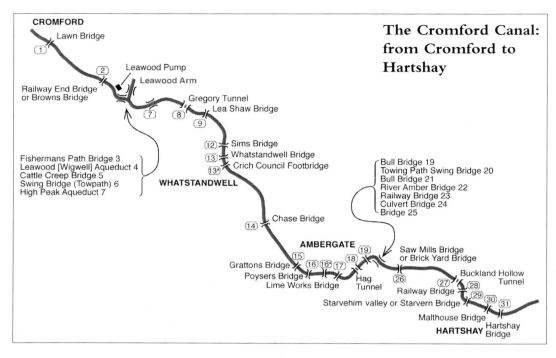

CROMFORD

The Cromford Canal: from Cromford to Hartshay

Lawn Bridge
①

② Leawood Pump
Leawood Arm

Railway End Bridge or Browns Bridge

⑦ ⑧ Gregory Tunnel
Lea Shaw Bridge
⑨

Fishermans Path Bridge 3
Leawood [Wigwell] Aqueduct 4
Cattle Creep Bridge 5
Swing Bridge (Towpath) 6
High Peak Aqueduct 7

⑫ Sims Bridge
⑬ Whatstandwell Bridge
⑬ᴬ Crich Council Footbridge

WHATSTANDWELL

Bull Bridge 19
Towing Path Swing Bridge 20
Bull Bridge 21
River Amber Bridge 22
Railway Bridge 23
Culvert Bridge 24
Bridge 25

⑭ Chase Bridge

AMBERGATE ⑲

⑮ ⑯ ⑯ᴬ ⑰ ⑱ Saw Mills Bridge or Brick Yard Bridge

Grattons Bridge
Poysers Bridge
Lime Works Bridge
Hag Tunnel
⑳ ⑳ Buckland Hollow Tunnel
⑳ ⑳ Railway Bridge
Starvehim valley or Starvern Bridge ⑳ ⑳ ⑳

Malthouse Bridge
HARTSHAY Hartshay Bridge

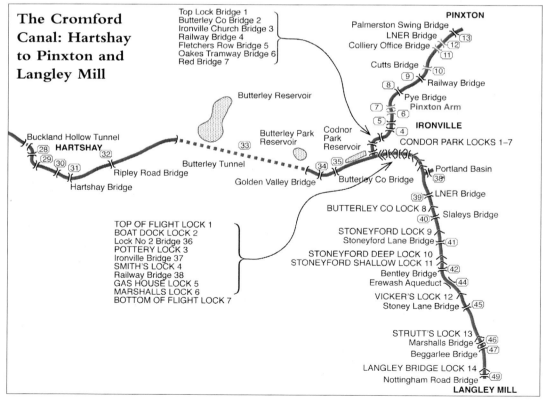

The Cromford Canal: Hartshay to Pinxton and Langley Mill

Top Lock Bridge 1
Butterley Co Bridge 2
Ironville Church Bridge 3
Railway Bridge 4
Fletchers Row Bridge 5
Oakes Tramway Bridge 6
Red Bridge 7

PINXTON

Palmerston Swing Bridge
LNER Bridge ⑬
Colliery Office Bridge ⑫
⑪

Cutts Bridge ⑩
⑨ Railway Bridge
⑧
Pye Bridge
⑦ ⑥ Pinxton Arm
⑤ **IRONVILLE**
④
CONDOR PARK LOCKS 1–7

Butterley Reservoir

Butterley Park Reservoir

Codnor Park Reservoir

Buckland Hollow Tunnel
⑳ **HARTSHAY** ⑳
⑳ ⑳ ⑳
Ripley Road Bridge
Butterley Tunnel
Golden Valley Bridge
Butterley Co Bridge
Hartshay Bridge

㉝
㉞ ㉟

Portland Basin ㊳
LNER Bridge
BUTTERLEY CO LOCK 8 ㊴
㊵ Slaleys Bridge

STONEYFORD LOCK 9
Stoneyford Lane Bridge ㊶

STONEYFORD DEEP LOCK 10
STONEYFORD SHALLOW LOCK 11 ㊷
Bentley Bridge
Erewash Aqueduct ㊹

VICKER'S LOCK 12
Stoney Lane Bridge ㊺

TOP OF FLIGHT LOCK 1
BOAT DOCK LOCK 2
Lock No 2 Bridge 36
POTTERY LOCK 3
Ironville Bridge 37
SMITH'S LOCK 4
Railway Bridge 38
GAS HOUSE LOCK 5
MARSHALLS LOCK 6
BOTTOM OF FLIGHT LOCK 7

STRUTT'S LOCK 13 ㊻
Marshalls Bridge ㊼
Beggarlee Bridge

LANGLEY BRIDGE LOCK 14
Nottingham Road Bridge ㊾
LANGLEY MILL

Introduction

By the end of the 1780s, the backbone structure of the English waterway system was in place, linking the four main river basins: Severn, Mersey, Trent and Thames. This became known as Brindley's Grand Cross, after the famous canal engineer James Brindley. From the Trent near Long Eaton, the Erewash Canal led northwards to Langley Mill, giving the collieries of the lower Erewash valley access to markets, particularly in the Leicester area via the River Soar. There were, however, many more coal mines further up the Erewash valley, and it was the need for an outlet for their products that brought about the concept of the Cromford Canal.

Initially, the proprietors of the Erewash Canal declined to co-operate, so there was a plan for a separate navigation using the Derwent from Derby, and its tributary, the Amber. However, this soon changed to an extension of the Erewash Canal from Langley Mill, with a branch to Pinxton. Engineer William Jessop estimated the cost at £42,697 in December 1788 (around £3 million today), although, as with almost all canal schemes of the time, this was to prove a gross underestimate. By the time of completion, this sum had effectively doubled. There was still opposition from the Erewash proprietors, but quite why is hard to understand. Apparently they feared a loss of water from the River Erewash, and yet any water taken from that river by the Cromford would end up in their canal, as would any additional water that the Cromford might abstract from the Derwent or elsewhere. They also stood to gain toll revenue, as goods reaching Langley Mill would continue by the Erewash Canal. The Nottingham Canal, which was later to join the Cromford at Langley Mill, was not yet a threat.

The line had great potential, not only from coal mines but from lead smelting plants at Lea, limestone and gritstone quarries around Crich and Lea, and the ironworks at Alderwasley. Often added to this list is Sir Richard Arkwright's cotton mills at Cromford. However, there is no evidence that cotton was carried to these mills by canal (it would have been a circuitous route from Liverpool by inland waterway) and, being water-powered, they had no need of coal.

Opposite above and below: The names of bridges and locks have changed over the years. Those given opposite are taken from an LMS Railway map of the 1930s/40s, the last years of commercial use for most of the canal.

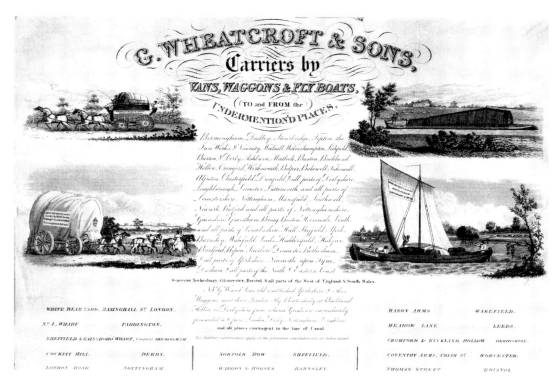

From the earliest days of the canal, Wheatcroft & Sons were the main long-distance carriers. Based at Buckland Hollow, the intersection of two major turnpike routes, they operated time-tabled services to Derby, Nottingham, Leicester, Birmingham and London, carrying all manner of light or perishable goods. Bulk cargoes such as coal and stone were initially transported by other carriers. (TWT/B)

Arkwright was involved, however, but by invitation. The promoters needed a respected name to lend credibility locally and to further their Act in the House of Commons, especially with the opposition it was receiving. In this, they were assisted by another respected local family, the Gells. Philip Gell of Hopton Hall near Wirksworth, owned mining and quarrying rights in the area, and his brother Captain John Gell had an office in London, from where he canvassed support and reported on parliamentary proceedings. Other land-owning supporters with local industrial interests included the Hurts of Alderwasley and Reverend d'Ewes Coke of Pinxton.

Another group of the promoters, namely Benjamin Outram, William Jessop, Francis Beresford and John Wright, formed the Butterley Company to exploit the reserves of coal and iron ore beneath Butterley Hill, through which the canal was to pass in an almost 3,000-yard-long tunnel. The only ingredient missing to make iron was limestone flux, and this was available at Crich, close to where the canal would pass. It was to be brought by tramway down to the canal at Bullbridge and loaded into boats for transport to Butterley. To its credit, in 2003 this company was still operating from the same site at Butterley under the same name, making similar large-scale iron and steel products. Indeed, the company built the spectacular Falkirk Wheel for the Scottish Lowland waterways in 2002.

There was more opposition in Parliament, particularly from the mill owners on the Derwent and from Derby Corporation, the latter fearing loss of trade as much as loss of water. There were problems too with Arkwright, who was not always the ardent supporter the promoters had hoped for. From the outset he began quibbling over water rights for his mills. He then refused to support the canal, unless the proposed water supply was changed from the Cromford Sough to a raised weir on the Derwent above his Masson Mill. From here, water would flow across his land where later Willersley Castle was built, cross the river on an aqueduct, and so feed the canal which would terminate nearer the river in what is now Cromford Meadows.

However, the Act was passed on 15 July 1789. William Jessop was appointed principal engineer, although his work had begun with surveys in 1787, and Benjamin Outram became superintendent of works. Thomas Sheasby and Thomas Dadford were appointed contractors for the whole canal, but were insolvent by 1791 and Outram was called in to complete the work using a direct labour force.

The canal was open to Pinxton by June 1792, but the opening to Cromford was delayed. Butterley Tunnel was behind schedule, and the long earth embankment and aqueducts across the road and river at Bullbridge were found to be unstable early in 1792. Then, towards the end of 1793, the spandrel walls of the stone aqueduct over the Derwent at Leawood partially collapsed. A second massive buttress was added to the south face to rectify this. Jessop blamed the failure on his use of Crich lime for the mortar – this was supposedly too pure to set. However, Schofield in his excellent biography of Outram suggests that there was something more fundamentally wrong in the design of this unusually long (80ft) span on a rise of only 20ft. The canal finally opened throughout in August 1794.

Despite Arkwright's ideas, the plans for supplying water from the Derwent were abandoned and the feed was taken from the Cromford Sough and Bonsall Brook. The reservoirs above Butterley Tunnel, which are today associated with the Cromford Canal, were in fact built for the later Nottingham Canal to ensure its water supply, but also, very conveniently, supplied the locks on the Cromford en route.

The private Leawood Arm was opened in 1802 linking mills, lead smelters and stone quarries at Lea with the main canal just south of Leawood or Wigwell Aqueduct. On the opposite side of the canal, from 1831, the Cromford & High Peak Railway effectively made the canal a through route, with considerable trade to Manchester.

The canal flourished and traffic soon built up to around 300,000 tons per year, a figure maintained until the 1850s. However, from the 1840s competition from railways caused the canal company to lower its tonnage rates (the amount charged per ton per mile) so that toll income began to fall rapidly – from £12,086 in 1841 to £7,588 in 1850. Share dividends dropped by half from their peak of over 20 per cent. As a result, in August 1852, it was decided to sell the canal to the Manchester, Buxton, Matlock & Midlands Junction Railway for £103,500. Trade immediately began to decline, halving by 1870, when the whole became part of the Midland Railway. It had fallen to less than 46,000 tons by 1888, with an increasing proportion of it being local rather than long-distance traffic.

Through traffic ceased in 1889 following a collapse in Butterley Tunnel, which was not repaired until 1893. Some 180 boats per year then used it, carrying 3-4,000 tons, until a second collapse in 1900 closed it for good. However, traffic continued between Pinxton and the main canal system, and coal was still carried on the now-isolated upper section from Hartshay to Lea and Cromford. The whole canal – apart from the half mile above Langley Mill which was still in use – was officially abandoned in 1944.

In the late 1960s British Waterways, who were then responsible for the derelict canal, began selling off sections: north of Langley Mill and between Hartshay and Buckland Hollow for open casting; at Sawmills to local householders and businesses; at Bullbridge to Stevenson's Dyers; at Ambergate to East Midlands Gas; and between there and Cromford to Derbyshire County Council (DCC) for a walking, cycling and wildlife trail.

CROMFORD CANAL.

36— PERMIT *Rob White* on board *Wheat & Son* Boat, No. —
to navigate the under-mentioned GOODS :

SPECIES.	Where loaded.	Where landed.	Weight by Bill of Lading.	Dry Inches	Tonnage Weight.	Miles.	Rate per Ton	AMOUNT. L. s. D.
Goods *Bun.*		*B. Hollon*	—	*Invoice*	3½	8	4/	5 1½
" "		*Pinxton*	1½	—	1½	6	2/3	1 10½
" *L Mill*		*Crompo*	—	—	3/6	15	3/6	1. 10½
								8. 10⅞

CROMFORD CANAL.

36¾ PERMIT *Sam.l Mather* on board *G. W. & Sons* Boat, No. 12
to navigate the under-mentioned GOODS :

SPECIES.	Where loaded.	Where landed.	Weight by Bill of Lading.	Dry Inches.	Tonnage Weight.	Miles.	Rate per Ton	AMOUNT. L. s. D.
Goods *Nott.*		*Crompo*	1622	8	15		7/6	1 2
" "		*Railway* 6			4	14	3/4	10 4
" "		*Hartstars* 1			1	12	2/8	2 3
" "		*B. Bridge* 1			1	9	4/9	1 9
								1. 16. 4

A page from a 'Permit' book showing the toll paid for cargo passing through Langley Mill.

Today, the whole route is walkable. The most interesting sections are: the bottom lock at Langley Mill, reopened in 1973 thanks to the Erewash Canal Preservation & Development Association (ECPDA); the bottom of Ironville locks to the eastern portal of Butterley Tunnel; the western portal to Hartshay; and the 5.5 miles between Ambergate and Cromford, restored by the erstwhile Cromford Canal Society and now owned and maintained by DCC. An accolade to the canal's historic importance is the inclusion of this last section in the UNESCO Derwent Valley Mills World Heritage Site.

Restoration at Langley Mill is gradually creeping northwards, and the formation of the Friends of the Cromford Canal (see page 128) offers hope for complete restoration.

Our historic journey along the canal takes us from Cromford to Langley Mill, then along the two arms, with the final chapters looking at the restoration work carried out in more recent years.

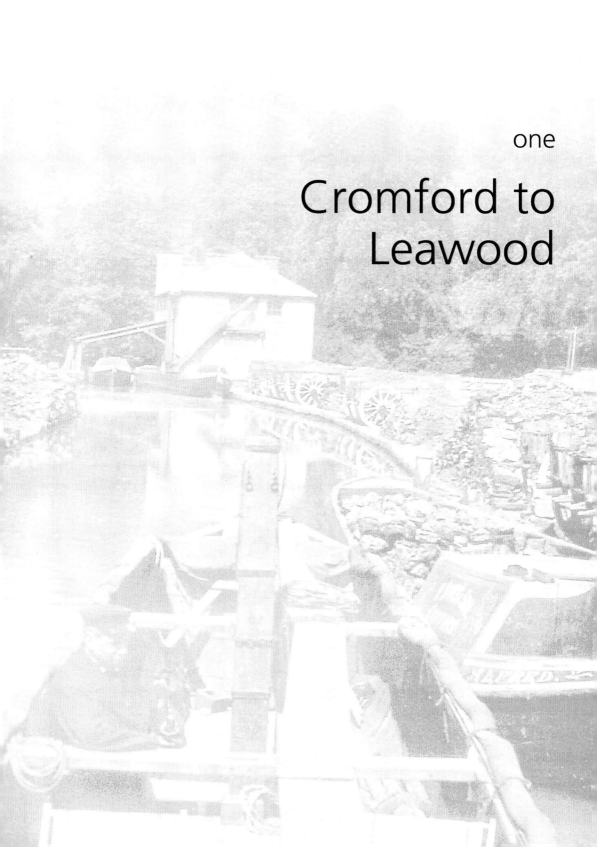

one
Cromford to
Leawood

When Henry Rodolph de Salis toured the canals for his seminal work *Bradshaw's Canals & Navigable Rivers of England & Wales*, he recorded his journeys in a diary with photographs. We are lucky that the photographs still survive in the collection of Hugh McKnight, who has kindly permitted the reproduction of some of the six taken on the Cromford Canal. Here, in 1897, de Salis' boat *Tipton* arrives at Cromford Wharf. Dawes & Son's *Alfred* awaits unloading whilst two other boats lie empty at the very end of the wharf. (Hugh McKnight)

In August 1906, the narrowboats *Onward* and *Bristol* lie at Cromford Wharf with huge lumps of coal neatly stacked, and the carts lined up waiting to deliver it locally. The operation was run by Wheatcrofts and continued up until the Second World War, despite this section of the canal being isolated from the main system by the final collapse of Butterley Tunnel in 1900. The coal came from Pentrich and Hartshay pits, to the west of the tunnel. Before the railways offered competition, Wheatcrofts had been based at Buckland Hollow, from where they operated fast and regular services carrying all kinds of goods. They later moved to Cromford, where they concentrated on the coal business. When boat traffic finally ceased, they brought the coal in by road. The original 'gothic' warehouse is to the left with its crane attached to the near-left corner, whilst to the right is the roof of the Agent's house and, beyond that, Arkwright's church. (TWT/B)

In an obviously posed photograph, W. Dawes & Son's boat *Shamrock* waits to be unloaded at Cromford Wharf. The large pieces of coal from previous deliveries have been individually man-handled off the boats and neatly stacked on the edge of the wharf. Horses and carts wait on the right to distribute the coal locally. In twelve months during 1900–1901, Dawes brought 176 boatloads of coal to Cromford, almost all from Hartshay. (SS)

In stark contrast, in March 1963 the wharf was totally devoid of boats, but not of freight traffic. As well as the odd wreck, the yard was well populated by lorries including at least one tanker specially designed to carry limestone filler, probably from the nearby Dene Quarry. The coal business was still active on the wharf to the left. (IM)

Left: The name of Wheatcroft was associated with the Cromford Canal for over 150 years. In fact this sign, or possibly a replica, was still in place at Cromford Wharf in 2003, over 200 years after the canal was opened. Seen here in the early years of the twentieth century, Nathaniel Wheatcroft's staff are well turned out for the photographer. (SS)

Below: When the canal was opened in 1794, there was a single terminal basin, preceded by a 'winding hole', where boats could turn round, as seen on this 1811 map. The canal runs beneath the words 'Cromford Wharf' to the right, whilst the Wirksworth to Nottingham Turnpike road runs up the map with the canal's water supply running alongside it at the bottom. From the southern wharf boundary this was culverted to the end of the basin close to the letter 'A', opposite the 'Gothic' warehouse pictured opposite. Because of the volume of trade, a second arm and warehouse were built, south of the first, to give the layout that we have today. The Agent's house and the boundary of Cromford Wharf to the north of the basin can still be seen. The unmarked building to the south is Rock House where Arkwright lived and through the grounds of which the canal was built. To the north is Arkwright's chapel and the road bridge across the River Derwent.

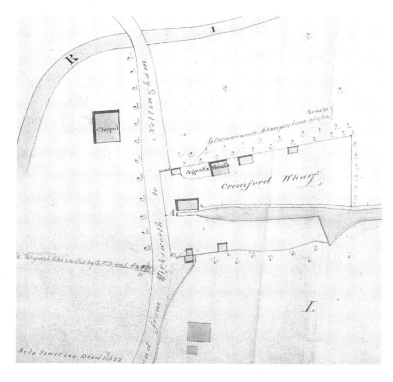

The scene at Cromford Wharf has changed little since this photograph was taken on 30 June 1963, even down to the cast-iron posts in the foreground. The 'Gothic' castellations which give this first warehouse its common name were probably included at the insistence of Sir Richard Arkwright, to enhance the view across the River Derwent from Willersley Castle – the place he had intended to become his home. In the event he died before Willersley was completed and before the canal opened. Large gates formerly closed off the entrance to keep the wharf secure. (BL)

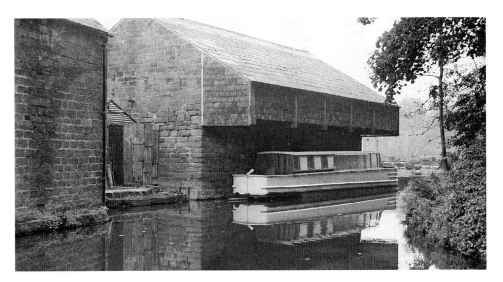

This October 1986 scene shows the Cromford Canal Society's trip boat *Marjorie A*, tied by the second warehouse. It is under a canopy designed to keep goods dry when being loaded or unloaded. The feed from Cromford Sough and Bonsall Brook was channelled into this second arm, although the culverted supply to the end of the original basin was maintained to keep the water there fresh. It ran beneath the now-demolished tin shed between the offices on the left, which may be those shown on the map of 1811 opposite, and the warehouse.

Close to where the two terminal arms split is a small boat house, with steps to the right. It is believed to have been built for Sir Richard Arkwright, whose home, Rock House, can be seen through the trees in this 1970s' view. The canal was cut through his gardens after some acrimonious discussions between Sir Richard and the Cromford Canal committee. The boat house is still in good condition, but the entrance and steps are usually obscured by ivy. (LW)

From what is now called High Peak Junction, the Cromford & High Peak Railway (CHPR) was opened through to the Peak Forest Canal at Whaley Bridge in 1831. This remarkable route was originally planned as a canal but it was soon realised that the limestone over which it passed would never hold water. A railway was built instead, on the planned canal line, with long level stretches linked by inclines. On 30 June 1963, a line of wagons and water tenders stands alongside the canal by Railway End or Brown's Swing Bridge no. 2. (BL)

Beyond the wagons in the preceeding photograph stood this small locomotive shed. In 1953 it had an air of abandonment, although the railway continued in operation until 1967. The side doors onto the canal suggest that it was designed for goods to be transhipped between wagons and boats before the extension of the CHPR was built in 1853 to join the Midland main line. It was doubtless succeeded in its purpose by the larger transhipment shed that still exists a few hundred yards to the south (page 20), beside the track of the former extension to the main line. (Roger Butler)

On 10 September 1928, the resident steam locomotive stands by the CHPR workshops. The two water tanks to its left were not only for topping up the engine's boiler but also for filling the tenders seen in the photograph opposite, to deliver water to other locomotive depots and isolated houses on the railway's route. Restored in 1985, the railway workshops can be visited and are the second oldest in the world. A small shop offers books and refreshments, plus an excellent audio tour of the area for hire. (Glynn Waite)

On 30 June 1963, this fine sign was still in place close to Bridge 2, despite the canal having been taken over by British Transport Waterways (BTW) at nationalisation in 1947, then by British Waterways on 1 January 1963. The remains of the sign are in the High Peak Junction workshops. (BL)

To the west of Swing Bridge 2 lies this warehouse, seen on 28 August 1981, with a crane base in the foreground. Wagons entered through the end doors to load or unload and could pass right through to the canopy beyond, which extends over the canal to keep cargo dry when transhipping. A common cargo in the early years of the railway was flour, brought by boat from Nottingham, travelling onward by train towards Manchester. The sign prohibits engines from entering the shed – due to the fire risk in the timber beams and floors. Today, known as the Wharf Shed, it is run by Derbyshire County Council as a bunk house for visiting groups.

As the CHPR had been planned as a canal, all its stations were originally called wharfs, so what is now called High Peak Junction was also known as Cromford Wharf – rather confusing to canal folk! Under the warehouse canopy in around 1920 stands the father-in-law of the late Victor Edge, for many years foreman joiner here. Two boats, of very different construction, apparently drift in the canal whilst the photographer takes his picture. (SS)

Seen from the canal towpath, 0–6–0T no. 58850, of North London Railway origin, shunts a Derbyshire stone wagon on 10 October 1951. High Peak Junction, in railway terms, was a mile to the left, where in 1853 the branch line linked the CHPR to what became the Midland Railway's main line. After this the CHPR no longer had to rely on the canal for its trade. (F.W. 'Tim' Shuttleworth)

Only a short distance from the Wharf Shed is Leawood Pump House, seen in this early twentieth-century view from the far side of Wigwell Aqueduct. The photographer is looking back past the swing bridge by the junction with the Leawood Arm, across the aqueduct to the pump house, beyond which are the buildings of High Peak Junction. Half-way to the swing bridge is what appears to be a windlass (see page 34) by the towpath, where today there is a run-off sluice. The pump was built in 1849 to raise water from the Derwent to the canal after supplies from Cromford Sough decreased, following the opening of Meerbrook Sough. This drained not only the deeper lead mines but also the water from the earlier sough. (SS)

For many years, the rotting remains of an ice-breaker were visible just above the surface of the canal opposite Leawood Pump (see page 2). When the canal was drained for repair work in the 1980s, the extent of decay was revealed, notably to the wood above water level. The sturdy construction can still be appreciated. The metal plating around the waterline, which prevented the ice cutting into the wood, has rusted and is peeling off. Remarkably, when the canal was refilled, the boat floated and the hull was towed to Cromford Wharf, but it was never restored. (LW)

Left: By 30 June 1963, the engine in Leawood Pump House was not being maintained and is seen to be well rusted in this view of the main steam cylinder. When operating, this produces the vacuum which lifts up the weighted pump rod at the other end of the huge cast iron beam. When the beam descends under its own weight, it expels over 3 tons of river water into the canal on each stroke. Before its restoration, it was thought to have last steamed around 1930. Restoration work was carried out by the Cromford Canal Society and the first public steaming was held on 4 August 1979. (BL)

No-one knows who this fine gentleman is, apparently in charge of the engine around the turn of the century when it was in regular operation. The control rods that he stands in front of are virtually unchanged today. (SS)

Left: The magnificent edifice of Leawood Pumping Station has changed little since it was built. The engine itself was built by Graham & Company at the Milton Iron Works, Elsecar. Today it is fully restored, maintained by a dedicated team of volunteers, and is in steam and open to the public on several weekends each summer when it is well worth a visit. (LW)

After the demise of the Cromford Canal Society, whose members are seen stoking one of the two boilers in 1979, maintenance of the Leawood Pump was taken over by a keen group of enthusiasts who were running the Middleton Top engine. This still operates, albeit by compressed air, on the former Cromford & High Peak Railway. Both of Leawood's boilers can be operated, and a weekend's steaming uses about 2 tons of coal – at a cost of around £100 per ton. Needless to say, donations are appreciated. As there is no road access to the pump house, the coal is delivered to the wharf opposite, and loaded into a boat for carriage across the canal – so the Cromford Canal can be said to be still carrying the traffic for which it was built!

Above: Wigwell Aqueduct across the River Derwent at Leawood caused Jessop problems during construction when it 'slumped'. He blamed this on the Crich lime used in the mortar being too pure to set. These icicles testify that it was still leaking in the 1960s. In 1984, Derbyshire County Council, with help from the Cromford Canal Society, spent £25,000 to line it with a tough black plastic 'Schlegel' membrane, which can still be seen today just above the water level. The main arch spans 80ft with only a 20ft rise. (FR)

Right: If you take the path down the south side of Wigwell Aqueduct to the River Derwent, you will see this stone set centrally above the main arch in anticipation of its completion date. In fact the slippage that occurred delayed opening until 1794. If you look carefully you may be able to make out a second, smaller, date stone below the larger one. The reason for there being two is not known. (BK)

This view from the hillside above the A6 shows the Derwent or Wigwell Aqueduct with Leawood
Pump House to its left and the canal snaking away past the Wharf Shed towards the railway workshops.
The broad elliptical span of Jessop's Aqueduct takes the canal across the Derwent and the massive
abutments either side can just be made out. On the outside of these were two smaller arches for
fishermen and cattle. At the far right of the aqueduct is the junction with the Leawood Arm (see page
105), which followed the river bank then headed away towards the hat factory and Smedley's mills, seen
in the middle distance above the aqueduct. (BK)

The much photographed cottage at the junction of the Leawood, or Nightingale, Arm was never so well captured as in this image by local photographer Frank Rodgers. The cottages were originally two dwellings and were almost certainly built for the use of Peter Nightingale's staff who were responsible for the lock at the entrance to this private arm, built by 1802. Complicated disputes over water rights caused the arm to be reduced to half its original length, but specific restrictions as to maintenance of water levels and access by boats necessitated the lock being manned. From contemporary reports, it is thought that a full length lock must have existed here at one time, but inspection of the site today suggests there was a pair of gates pointing in opposite directions to maintain higher water at either side.

The last known resident of the cottage was Mr Bowler, seen here crossing the aqueduct probably to collect his drinking water from beside the railway. He lived alone as a recluse in Aqueduct ('Ackerduck' to the locals) Cottage around 1950-70. Note the simple plank bridge across the main canal where the swing bridge has now been reinstated. After he left, there were various attempts to use the cottage as a walkers' bunk house and fisherman's lodge, but eventually vandalism took its toll. (FR)

Opposite below: The well-painted LMSR maintenance boat *Thistle* at the entrance to the Leawood Arm in front of Aqueduct Cottage in the 1930s. The swing bridge is open to allow the boat to pass. Holding the tiller is Edward Sampson, inspector for this section of the canal until his retirement in 1958. He had joined the old Midland Railway before its amalgamation in 1923 and lived in Whatstandwell. (Hilda Scrimshaw)

Left: Mrs Ann Eaton sits outside Aqueduct Cottage, where she lived for many years, with one of her daughters, Mrs Violet Farnsworth, and her two children Henrietta and Arthur. They are sitting on the steps from which they drew washing water from the canal. The cottage had no mains services. (Ivy Turberville)

Below: Aqueduct Cottage in autumn 1905, photographed by William Henry Stockwell. The small wooden swing bridge over the entrance to the Leawood Arm can be seen crossing the narrows where once were housed stop gates to control the water level in the side arm and to prevent loss of water from the main canal. (Julie Simpson)

two

Leawood
to Ambergate

Above: In February 1989, after severe storms and melting snow had blocked run-offs, the canal overtopped its bank between Leawood and Gregory Tunnel with this result. Fortunately new piling installed by the Cromford Canal Society ensured that it did not breach. Ever since the canal was first built, there had been problems with slippage on this section. It was mentioned in the company minutes of 1801, and a major breach occurred in 1920, as seen on pages 31 and 32. (SS)

Left: This unusual view of the cast iron aqueduct carrying the canal over the Midland Railway was taken from on top of the adjacent Leawood railway tunnel. Beyond the canal, the line crosses the Derwent before reaching the 'real' High Peak Junction, where the Cromford & High Peak Railway joined the main line from 1853. The canal to the right contours round the spur of land, Lea Wood, through which the railway tunnels. There was a second aqueduct as the track emerged at the other end, carrying the Leawood Arm – see page 106. On top of the distant quarry face is Crich Stand, the memorial to the Sherwood Foresters who died in the First World War. (FR)

The construction of the cast iron aqueduct over the railway, with its supporting diagonal across the side, and its plated base, could be seen when the canal was drained for dredging in the 1980s. A similar cast iron trough was used for the other two railway aqueducts on the Cromford Canal. However, whilst here the iron trough was left visible from the railway, at Bullbridge it was set into the embankment and on the Leawood Arm it was faced with ornamental stonework. (LW)

The length between the railway aqueduct and Gregory Tunnel was prone to slippage. This was brought home to the Midland Railway on 21 February 1920 when a large breach appeared in their canal. Fortunately, the water ran straight into the river, causing no damage to property or the nearby railway. On such a steep embankment, it was lucky that the water took out only a section of the bank, and did not wash away the whole canal bed as well. The canal was reopened on 20 April. (LK)

The most dramatic view of the 1920 breach was from below, at the level of the Derwent's flood plain. But where are all the workers? They appear to have downed tools and gone home, yet surely valuable equipment would not be left unattended? (LK)

Considering that the coal traffic from Hartshay to Cromford and Lea continued until just before the Second World War, it is surprising that there are not more photographs of it. In 1935 a group of lads hitched a ride on a pair of loaded boats, pulled by a single horse, and fortunately John Heydon had his camera with him to record the scene on board the boats, carrying 'nutty slack'. The largish amount of freeboard on the boats suggests that they were not fully loaded – probably reflecting the lack of dredging. It was normal practice in these last years of traffic on this canal for a single horse to pull two boats closely tied together. The boats are passing the site of the breach pictured above. (SS)

The first of four tunnels on the canal is Gregory Tunnel, 42 yards long, where Jessop decided to cut through the outcrop rather than contour round it as he did at Leawood. Despite having a towpath, the local author Alison Uttley, writing about her childhood memories from the 1890s, says that the horses were unhitched and walked over the top, whilst the boats were manhandled through, although this was not normal canal practice. (FR)

As the tunnel emerges from the hillside, the canal enters Gregory Wide Hole. When the canal's southern (right-hand) embankment was built, it acted as a dam to small local streams and created this elegant pool. The builders did not need to bother putting in any banking on the north side. In the 1840s, two boatbuilding docks were in business here. Along the canal can be seen Leashaw Farm, the hamlet of Robin Hood in the centre, and Dawbarns timber works in the distance by the River Derwent.

On this postcard titled 'Canal at Lea Shaw', the elegant lady is standing at the end of Gregory Wide Hole, just beyond a 'windlass' beside the towpath. In the canal bed lay a trap door covering an outlet to a culvert which drained to the river on the right. Attached to the door was a chain which normally lay on the canal bed. This could be attached to the roller on the windlass, which was then turned to hoist the trap door open and drain the canal for maintenance, or to release water in the case of a breach. (Roger Butler)

One of the boats shown on page 32 delivered its coal to Lea Wharf and was then hauled backwards, empty, to Gregory Wide to turn round. The sharpness of the junction with the Leawood Arm and the lack of width in the canal would not allow it to turn there. One might have imagined it would have been nearer and easier to turn just opposite Leawood Pump where there is sufficient width, but perhaps there was not enough depth at the time. (SS)

Because the canal ran so high up the side of the valley, it was essential to be able to close off sections of the canal in case of a breach. The conventional manual technique of inserting stop planks was good for planned maintenance, but no use for an emergency such as seen on the previous pages. In an attempt to provide gates that would automatically close, many canals adopted what have been dubbed 'Brindley Gates' after the famous canal engineer on whose canals they were first used. In the drawing below by Edward Paget-Tomlinson, we see the conjectural arrangement at Leashaw Bridge (9), where contractors relining the canal revealed parts of the gates during dredging. The gates pivoted across the width of the canal bed, which was stone lined in such places. If a breach occurred to the right of the bridge, the flow of water would force the left-hand gate to rise, thus blocking off any further flow, and vice versa. Indicative signs on the canal today are an elongated narrows such as at Leashaw and several other bridges, including Whatstandwell (above) where an additional tell-tale is the arched recess in the masonry, clearly visible from the towpath, inside which the gates would have rotated. In view of the canal now being in the Derwent Valley Mills World Heritage Site, it is to be hoped that one of these historic features can be properly excavated and recorded.

The hamlet of Robin Hood lies between Gregory Tunnel and Whatstandwell. The site was a stone saw mill, built there because of its proximity to Duke's Quarries (which supplied gritstone for the construction of buildings as far away as London) and water power offered by the stream which runs through the hamlet before passing under the canal in a deep culvert. In 1811, there was a stone wharf but no buildings. The lower floor of the house closest to the canal shows its original cast iron windows in this early twentieth-century view. A steam engine was once installed here, but is thought never to have operated, possibly because of the stone traffic being transferred from canal to railway. A short track was built from the quarries to the main line, crossing the canal at Sims Bridge. The canal is narrower now than seen here, and the workshop to the right is no longer there. (David Spray)

From having no buildings in the early-nineteenth century, the importance of the gritstone trade ensured that Robin Hood soon grew into this isolated hamlet, which today is idyllically situated by the canal overlooking the Derwent Valley. Many towpath walkers will have coveted the house by the canal that lies in its own private amphitheatre of a garden.

Between Robin Hood and Whatstandwell, Sims Bridge (12) used to carry the tramway from Duke's Quarries across the canal where stone was transferred to wagons on the main line railway which runs parallel to the canal, just to the right. The original decking was replaced by a lighter weight footbridge over a decade after this 1963 photograph was taken. (BL)

A postcard view of Whatstandwell. This village straggles out along the former turnpike road leading up the hill towards Crich from the Derwent Hotel by the river bridge (to the right) on what is now the A6. In 1811, the hotel was called The Ship, later the Bull's Head. Telegraph poles show the line of the railway. Around the time of the photograph, the house by the canal bridge was a shop.

Eden House at Whatstandwell is built directly over the short railway tunnel. In 1811 the house was part of Hurt's wharf, and it is thought that the owner refused to allow it to be knocked down when the railway was built, so the railway tunnelled under instead! Hurt was the Squire of Alderwasley, and also the proprietor of the iron forge between here and Ambergate by the River Derwent. (BK)

The tithe map of 1841 shows a wharf here at Whatstandwell on the opposite, northern, side of the canal to Eden House. In 1945 one of the last boats was tied up there, still floating and apparently in good condition, but looking somewhat neglected. As the local Canal Inspector Edward Sampson lived nearby until his retirement in 1958, this was a convenient and safe place to tie up the boat. (Fred Copeland)

In classic geography textbook fashion, river, road, railway and canal squeeze together into the valley, the latter two preferring to keep to a slightly higher contour. The cumbersomely-named Manchester, Buxton, Matlock & Midlands Junction Railway bought the canal in 1852. In 1870 it became part of the Midland Railway's main line from Derby to Manchester, which had opened in 1867, but is now a single track branch to Matlock, and even chartered steam trains are no longer permitted owing to lack of maintenance on bridges. With vegetation still well controlled in this early 1960s view, the express can be clearly seen as it heads south from Whatstandwell. (FR)

Many local people recall tales of Sunday School and church outings on scrubbed-out coal boats. Surprisingly, this is the only photograph of these events so far discovered. According to local memories, churches around Ripley ran trips to Cromford and vice versa! (Miss A. Dunn)

Like most canal companies, Cromford's was obliged to install milestones. They were to indicate the mileage from each end so that correct tolls could be charged for cargoes carried. These were calculated at so many pence per ton per mile. Two original stones survive *in situ*. This one indicates 'Langley 11 miles'. The other side states 'Cromford 3½ miles', the conventional figure 'one' of the half being replaced by a small circular mark. Both are, unusually, on the offside of the canal. At some later date, small concrete posts were installed every half mile, usually beside the towpath, and several of these remain.

Although quite a well-known postcard image, this is the only photograph from this era depicting a boat at work on the once busy canal. Taken before 1905, it shows a well-laden boat, carrying 25-30 tons, passing beneath Chase Bridge. Such boats were the standard 'narrowboats' of the Midlands canals, 70ft long and 7ft wide. In comparison with the later photographs where a horse tows two boats, here there is just a single boat. No doubt the canal was better dredged at this time giving a greater depth of water, and enabling each boat to carry more coal.

This pre-1905 postcard again shows Chase Bridge (14), with a boat tied up to the small wharf beyond, probably awaiting a load of gritstone from the nearby quarries. In most photographs of this bridge, the stop planks are in the holders to the left, but here they are clearly missing – perhaps in place under the bridge for some reason. Crich Chase is the large area of land above the canal to the north, formerly a royal hunting ground. (BK)

Proving that kids will always be kids, this image from the 1920s shows children on board a former ice-breaker, apparently relegated to maintenance duties. On the bows the raised lettering 'LM&SR' is attached, indicating the then owners of the canal, the London, Midland & Scottish Railway. The original was taken on what appears to be a tin plate negative, which has become damaged over the years, hence the poor state of the picture. The most likely location is thought to be Poyser's Bridge (16) at Ambergate. This is where Chase Road crosses the canal and so is sometimes confused with Chase Bridge (14) above. (Fred Copeland)

Known by many as St John's Cottages these canalside buildings, prominently visible from the A6 just north of Ambergate, bore the St John's logo for many years when they were an outdoor centre. In earlier years they had provided accommodation for three families, and before that they were Hay's Wharf. The mooring rings can still be seen in the coping stones. Just before the turn of the century, a Mr Elliott set up a grocery business in the farthest building (which still has a large shop-style window facing the canal) and sold to both locals and the canal people. He later moved his business into Ambergate village itself.

The rural charm of Poyser's Bridge (16) is captured in this undated painting by Frances M. Ellis of Alfreton. What a contrast this scene of Crich Chase Farm must have been with Ambergate Lime Works, just round the corner. The buildings and bridge still stand, but the 'mountains' in the background have to be put down to artistic licence. The Poyser family were local landowners in the nineteenth century. (Gordon Lee)

three

Ambergate
to Butterley

Above: Just around the corner from the last scene at Ambergate, George Stephenson & Company built these lime kilns in 1840-41. They burned Crich lime using coal discovered when cutting Clay Cross Tunnel on the North Midland Railway, for which George Stephenson was engineer. Depicted here not long after opening, they were later altered in form. They remained in use until the 1960s, the limestone being brought down the hillside from Crich by a metre-gauge mineral railway. The canal lies invisible on their far side and the railway crossed it to reach the top of the kilns. This was first horse, then locomotive, hauled on the level sections. The main difference in height was overcome by a 1-in-4 rope-operated counterbalanced incline, controlled by a huge brake drum. As far as is known the works never used the canal for transport; Stephenson, and what was to become the Clay Cross Company, naturally preferred the railway. The works were connected by sidings on either side of the kilns to the main North Midland line.

Opposite above: The Ambergate lime kilns ceased operation in 1965. This aerial view was taken early in the following year, just before work began for East Midlands Gas Board's 'reforming' plant, which was to totally reprofile the site and destroy the canal. The line of Stephenson's incline ('The Steep') can be seen from top left to centre of the picture. There are some wagons at the bottom by the bridge over the canal, which runs from left to right across the centre. To the right the canal makes a sharp turn to enter the short Hag (sometimes spelt Hagg) Tunnel rather than contour round the outcrop. Above this the line of the canal can just be made out as it passes under the Derwent Valley Aqueduct pipeline, now within the boundary of Stevenson's dye works. The snow-covered rail line in front of the kilns met the sidings from the main line at right angles, wagons being transferred by a turntable.

Opposite below: George Stephenson died in 1848, and in 1852 the company changed its name to the Clay Cross Company. In an attempt to improve efficiency, the stone chimneys were removed and replaced by round steel pre-heaters on the seven eastern kilns in 1910. Soon after, the company produced a series of promotional postcards of which this is one. The railway from the quarries at Crich crossed the canal to reach the hoist seen to the left of the pre-heaters, from where the limestone was transferred to the kilns. Burnt lime was loaded onto wagons at the base of the kilns.

CLAY CROSS Cos KILNS AT AMBERGATE WHERE "CRICH" LIME IS PRODUCED

The railway bridge from the bottom of 'The Steep' to the Ambergate lime kilns is seen from on top of the massive stockpile of limestone on the north side of the canal. A branch of the metre-gauge railway penetrates a short way into the stone. On the far side of the canal, some unburnt limestone was transferred to main line railway wagons for transport to the Clay Cross blast furnaces. (Cliff Williams)

This view to the left of the photograph above shows the post-1910 'upgraded' lime kilns. On the left is the 1841 coal wagon hoist powered by a stationary steam engine until 1948. Between the kilns and canal is a branch siding of the North Midland Railway upon which wagons appear to be loaded with unburnt limestone. (Cliff Williams)

One of the reasons for the choice of site for the EMGas reforming plant was the fact that the land was already in industrial use and so planning permission for this massive project was not difficult to obtain. For those who know the site today, it may come as a surprise to see this view from January 1969. The line of the canal was just in front of the large cylindrical gas storage tanks on the left. The complexity of the site and its infrastructure explain why such a large area of land was needed. Ironically, the plant only operated for a few years before becoming redundant. The site is now a major pipeline manufacturing and storage depot for Transco, who maintain the United Kingdom's gas pipeline grid. (HD)

The 92-yard Hag Tunnel cut through a small rocky spur and had a towpath running through it with a handrail. The north end was delightfully captured on film by Ernest Key around 1960. The southern portal was buried when the gas works were developed. (Joyce Key)

Although a rather poor photograph, this illustrates what happened to the canal at the northern end of Hag Tunnel. A massive concrete wall was built across the end and a large reservoir constructed for use by Stevenson's. The stones of the tunnel portal can still be seen above the reservoir. (Peggy Henson, Stevenson's Dyers)

From the hillside above, Bullbridge still has the appearance of a small hamlet in this photograph. The Canal Inn to the left and most of the buildings around the road bridge still survive, many now belonging to Stevenson's dye works. As the canal curves to the right, it passes the Bullbridge lime kilns, built at the same time as the canal to serve the Butterley Company. In 1860, 8,000 tons of burnt lime was supplied along with 30,000 tons of unburnt limestone. After crossing the aqueducts, the canal swings left through Sawmills.

The Canal Inn at Bullbridge, seen here from the canal in the early 1970s, remains largely unchanged today. (LW)

As the canal approached Bullbridge, it passed a 'narrows' where stop planks (seen stored on the right) could be inserted to block off the water and allow a section to be drained for maintenance. This would have been particularly important here as the canal is about to cross the long and always troublesome embankment over the river, railway and road. Note the skeletal form of the lime works that is fully clad in the picture opposite. These ceased operation around 1933.

Seen from the top of Stevenson's chimney, a former dry dock can be made out, bottom left, where boats were repaired up to the end of commercial traffic in the 1930s. In 1843 it belonged to Joseph Bowmer, and in the latter years was operated by the Key family. The dock and canal are now within Stevenson's site. The stop plank narrows are just out of view to the left. (George Smith Collection)

This image comes from a small crumpled snapshot that once belonged to Edward Sampson, Inspector for this length of canal until his retirement in 1958. It may well be him in the ice-breaker, which looks like it is being built from scratch on the dry dock at Bullbridge. The distinctive tall wall can be seen in the previous photograph. There is a striking resemblance between this photograph and John Constable's more famous painting of boat building in the dry dock by Flatford Mill. (Hilda Scrimshaw)

Above: Considering the devastation to the canal on either side, it is a surprise that this 1950s scene is totally recognisable today, even down to the water in the canal. The cottages to the right have been modernised to incorporate the stabling below, but the bridge is now obscured by trees and infilled beneath. Beyond the bridge (towards Cromford) is part of Stevenson's dye works and the line of the canal is a roadway. (John E. Lynam)

Right: Between Bullbridge and the aqueduct stood this delightful cottage, with its outhouses, beside the canal on what is now part of Stevenson's car park. As the canal swings right, part of the remains of the lime kilns – by this time long disused – can be seen. This was always a popular walk with locals so it was an even greater pity that the canal was drained and the aqueduct beyond demolished in 1968. (FR)

The first penetration of the Bullbridge embankment was for the track to the lime kilns, today called Drovers Way. When the road and railway aqueducts were demolished in autumn 1968, this smaller arch was spared. Seen here in January 1969, it survives today as part of the Grade II Listed embankment, although in 2002 planning permission was granted for a house to be built above it. Part of the lime kilns can be seen through the arch. (HD)

For all the modern equipment seen at the Bullbridge lime kilns in the earlier pictures, very little remained when it was photographed in the 1950s. Drovers Way crosses just in front of the ruins, having passed under the canal embankment to he left. Today, even less of the site remains as houses have been built on and around it. (FR)

In this view across the aqueduct, a Midland Railway 2P Class 4-4-0 locomotive is just about to pass under the canal heading towards Ambergate Junction. The Butterley Company's lime kilns are to the right. This is the only known photograph to show these kilns in any detail in their earlier operational state, probably soon after 1900 when they were raised by 10ft to increase capacity. It possibly predates the distant views on pages 47 and 48 as the massive superstructure appears not yet to have been erected. *(Nottingham Evening Post)*

Immediately above Drovers Way was this swing bridge, which enabled horses to cross the canal as the towpath changed sides here. Looking from Bullbridge to Sawmills, the number '21' can be seen on a characteristic cast iron plate in the centre of the span. By the late 1950s, the canal was in far worse condition than in the photograph above, being almost completely drained. In 2003, the cast iron deck plate of this Grade II Listed bridge lay broken at Cromford Wharf, where it was moved to around 1984. (FR)

This 'classic' shot of the aqueduct with boat and train is well known, but deserves publishing again. In the foreground is the Swing Bridge 21, around which the parapet wall above Drovers Way has been designed to curve. Beyond, the towpath continues on the left, with an unguarded path on the right. The boat with horse has no doubt paused on the aqueduct to allow the unknown photographer to capture the northbound express train just at the right moment. To the right of the boat is the tank, fed from the canal, which supplied water for the steam locomotives.

As the canal was there 'first', the Cromford Canal Company could dictate the terms for the construction of the railway, and stipulated that canal traffic should not be delayed. The railway company had Butterley iron works produce a cast iron tank 150ft long, 9ft wide and 6ft deep. It was conveyed to Bullbridge, presumably floating in the canal, in five parts and, starting at midnight on Saturday 2 March 1839, the parts were assembled, floated into position and sunk into place within twenty-four hours. Traffic on the canal was not disrupted as it was normally closed on Sundays. The bridge for the railway was subsequently dug out beneath the trough.

This earlier depiction of the canal across the railway was one of a series commissioned by Francis Thompson, architect for the North Midland Railway, at the time it opened in 1840. Although the architectural details are apparently accurate, the depiction of the masted sailing boat on this narrow canal has to be attributed to artistic licence. The water on the left is not the main River Amber (which crosses under the canal further to the left) but Bullbridge mill tail race which crossed under both railway and canal at this point. Note the accurately depicted tiny Gothic arch of the road aqueduct on the right, which was perfectly adequate for the horse-drawn carriages of the time.

The Bullbridge road aqueduct, seen in the top view, survived unaltered (apart from the addition of traffic lights) until the late 1960s when road widening was finally deemed a necessity. Despite a vigorous campaign by the Inland Waterways Protection Society to save the canal by widening the roadway beneath it, it was decided to completely demolish the historic structure, and the railway aqueduct adjacent, as well as one of the houses above. (FR)

The fateful day late in 1968 when the arch of the road aqueduct was finally demolished by Derbyshire County Council. It had been built for the turnpike era of horses and carriages, and it was remarkable that it had survived for so long. (Peggy Henson, Stevenson's Dyers)

Not long after the road arch was demolished, the railway span followed. Amongst the rubble lay some of the Butterley cast iron plates that were bolted together in 1839 to prefabricate the trough which held the canal water and allowed the railway to tunnel beneath. Similar construction is still evident on the surviving railway aqueduct at Leawood. (HD)

The towpath of the Cromford Canal was, and still is, a public right of way. After Bullbridge Aqueduct was demolished, the remaining embankment to the north-west was graded and a zig-zag path created. Seen here in January 1969, the embankment has since become almost completely overgrown with scrub. In the foreground is the point where the canal previously crossed the railway and walkers had to cross the lines. (HD)

At the south-eastern end of the aqueduct was a small shed, built out of railway sleepers, in which the canal maintenance gang stored their tools and brewed up. To the right was a dry dock, filled in around 1912. Maintenance work was still going on when this photograph was taken in the 1940s, and two well cared for boats are tied up by the shed. Mr J. Slack and Mr F. Beeson are standing on the towpath. (BK)

Many local people remember the boat *Thistle* that was abandoned to gradually decay at the south-eastern end of Bullbridge Aqueduct. In this photograph from the late 1950s, it is still in reasonable condition, although it is obviously going nowhere with the canal half drained. Note that despite the stop planks in place where the boy is sitting on the bank, there are still more in their holder to the left. (FR)

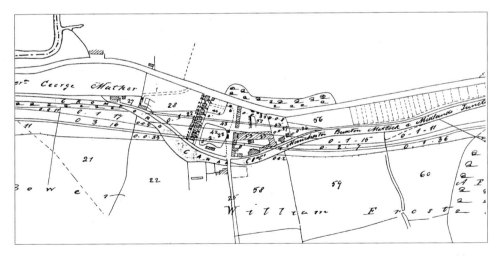

The Midland Railway branch line from Ambergate to Pye Bridge was opened in 1875. It would have crossed the canal twice in quick succession just east of Bullbridge, where rail and canal were on similar levels. Rather than raise the railway or have two lift bridges, the decision was taken to divert the Midland Railway-owned canal. As a result, the loop to the original Ridge Bridge (named after local landowner David Ridge) shown here was cut off and a new four-arched bridge built to span the canal and the railway. The new bridge was numbered 26 the old bridge 26A. The remains of one side of the old bridge arch are still visible. (Peter Free)

Above: The canal arch of the new Brickyard Bridge 26 in 1963, when this length of canal was still in water. All four arches of the bridge remain today, although the canal is infilled. The bridge gave access from the turnpike road (later the A610) to the Ambergate Brick & Tile Works, later General Refractories and now Lockwood's Haulage Depot whose new access road cuts through the bed of the realigned canal. (Reg Schofield)

Right: Parents today might have a fit seeing their children sitting so close to deep water, but such 'dangers' were accepted 100 years ago. Lewes and Percy are seen at the western entrance to Buckland Hollow Tunnel, the shortest on the canal at 32 yards and the only one without a handrail on the towpath. Although the canal is infilled today, you can still walk through the tunnel to the Excavator pub just beyond. On the left, alongside the towpath, were once Wheatcrofts' wharves and warehouses.

The narrowboat *Shamrock*, working in tandem with a second boat from which the photograph was taken, is pulled by a horse led by young Joe Poplar. They are heading, laden with coal, towards Cromford and have just passed under Starvehimvalley Bridge. Soon they will take the sharp left bend at Buckland Hollow, where the Excavator pub now stands. On the left is the mineral railway line from Upper Hartshay colliery to the Ambergate & Pye Bridge line at Buckland Hollow, the embankment of which can be made out on the right. (SS)

After Buckland Hollow and the curiously named but extant Starvehimvalley Bridge, the canal wandered across fields to what most locals called Martha's Bridge (30). Martha Clarke, was the proprietor of the nearby boarding house. On an 1811 map it is called Harty (Hartshay) Malthouse Bridge. The area was apparently known as Klondike but is totally untraceable today following opencasting. (Joyce Key)

One of the more bizarre stories associated with the canal concerns the locals of Hartshay who used to gather by the bridge for a chat and a smoke. One wet day in 1894, the owner of a canalside pigsty suggested that they cleaned it out and used it as reading rooms. This they did, later expanding into the adjacent pigsty. They charged members weekly and bought newspapers and books. The exact location is uncertain, but in this newspaper picture we see 'The President' outside the 'Reading Rooms', quite clearly beside the canal and a sunken boat. (Heather McKeurton)

Bridle Lane Bridge (31) at Hartshay seen from opposite Hartshay Wharf. The sunken boat is wooden, so is not the boat whose remains can be seen almost buried today. The houses on the left were built on the site of the former 'Brass Foundry', or Ripley Works, which produced brass and galvanised iron sheeting. It closed in 1885 and the main buildings and chimney were demolished in 1895. (Joyce Key)

Sadly this scene is not what it at first appears. The horse is not pulling the boats, for the iron boats are sunk, just to the east of Hartshay Wharf, the western part of which is seen in the photograph on the previous page. The railway wagons in the background are standing on the wharf on a line that linked to Upper Hartshay Colliery. The houses of Hartshay are lost in the misty background.

Also confusingly known as Hartshay Wharf, this short arm on the north side of the canal was accessed under a bridge carrying the main line towpath, from which this picture was taken. It lay just to the east of the main Ripley Road (Hartshay Hill) Bridge. The wharf originally received coal via horse-drawn plateways from an old colliery close to Pentrich village, but later a standard gauge line was put in to allow access to the Ambergate & Pye-Bridge branch of the Midland Railway, and also to the newer Pentrich Colliery at Hammersmith (now the site of Geeson's scrap yard). Pentrich – or Haslam's – colliery was sometimes called 'Shonker' pit. Notice the size and quality of the coal, which is being manhandled piece by piece and individually stacked in the boat in this photograph from around 1900. In the centre with the stick, standing between boat and wagon, is George Henry Key; next to him, standing in the boat, is Jack Key. The towpath bridge is now demolished, and the arm filled in to form part of the garden to the modernised wharf house. (Pat Morriss)

Opposite below: In June 1909, a none-too-happy line of men are hard at work by Ripley Road Bridge (32), Hartshay. The Gate Inn lies temptingly to the left! The bridge is the original structure, at the bottom of 'Hartshay Hill' on the main Ripley road. Traffic was such that it had to be replaced in the 1930s by the present wide flat-decked bridge, although an even greater increase in traffic more recently has caused a completely new A610 to be built across the canal behind the camera, and the road over the bridge is now a dead end. Rather than simply digging the canal deeper, it is thought that the work was to raise the canal banks which have subsided because of coal mining beneath. Evidence of such bank raising on the towpath is still visible. (LK)

The bridge carrying the towpath across the entrance to Hartshay Wharf, seen in the previous picture, looking towards the old Ripley Road Bridge in June 1909. Although Butterley Tunnel had been closed for nine years, the canal was still maintained as local coal traffic was carried to Lea and Cromford until the 1930s. The photograph was taken on the same day as the lower one on page 62. (LK)

Just to the east of Hartshay Wharf there is now a huge embankment carrying the A610 across the canal. In early 1976 the canal was completely excavated here and this reinforced concrete bed was laid, on which were run twin pipes to take the water, before the embankment was built. Two of these can be seen in the distance and, just to the right, the roof of the Hartshay wharf house. (Pat Morriss)

four

Butterley
Tunnel

The western portal as it was from 1890 until 1976, although looking rather overgrown on 30 August 1971. The portal was later incorporated into the 20-yard extension necessary for the construction of the A38 across the canal here.

Left: On 13 December 1964, a group of intrepid (some would say foolhardy) enthusiasts launched a small boat at the western end to explore the tunnel. Note that the water in the tunnel is some four stop planks higher than that outside, enabling their boat to float readily. It is thought the stop planks were in place to encourage water to flow towards the eastern end from where the canal supplied water to Codnor Park forge. The main feed from Butterley Reservoir, sited directly above the tunnel, was down a vertical shaft into the tunnel some 600 yards from this entrance. The story of this adventure was recounted in an article in the national inland waterway magazine *Waterways World* for August 2000. (Derek Gittings)

Opposite below: A well-posed photograph of a sturdily-built boat being 'legged' out of the tunnel on 30 April 1907. The massive piles of timber and cross beams are possibly for loading heavy machinery onto boats for use in the tunnel. Although closed as a through route by this time, there was still access to the Butterley Company's 'Wide Hole' (see pages 69–71) and possibly to local coal faces. The image has been adopted by the Friends of the Cromford Canal for their logo (page 128).

NOTICE.

EXTRACT FROM THE RULES, BYELAWS AND ORDERS MADE BY THE CROMFORD CANAL COMPANY: 30TH MAY 1804

NO BOAT SHALL ENTER BUTTERLEY TUNNEL AT THE EAST END EXCEPT BETWEEN THE HOURS OF FIVE AND SIX IN THE MORNING, ONE AND TWO IN THE AFTERNOON AND NINE AND TEN AT NIGHT AND NO BOAT SHALL ENTER THE WEST END THEREOF, EXCEPT BETWEEN THE HOURS OF ONE AND TWO IN THE MORNING, NINE AND TEN IN THE FORENOON AND FIVE AND SIX AT NIGHT, AND EVERY BOAT SHALL MAKE ITS PASSAGE THROUGH THE SAME WITH ALL POSSIBLE DESPATCH AND ON NO ACCOUNT EXCEED THREE HOURS AFTER SUCH ENTRY. AND IF ANY PERSON OR PERSONS HAVING THE CARE OF ANY BOAT, SHALL OFFEND IN ANY OF THE PARTICULARS AFORESAID, HE OR THEY SHALL FORFEIT FOR EVERY SUCH OFFENCE FORTY SHILLINGS AND SHALL ALSO TURN BACK ON MEETING ANOTHER BOAT IN THE SAID TUNNEL.

Butterley Tunnel was a problem for the Cromford Canal Company from the very beginning. It delayed the opening of the canal until 1794, and subsequently caused its closure as a through route on 6 June 1900. In the meantime, special arrangements had to be enforced for boats passing through the tunnel so that they did not meet in the middle. The tunnel was only 9ft wide, and the 'narrowboats' that used it were 7ft wide, so they could not pass each other. The regulations were displayed on boards at each end of the tunnel, although for whose benefit is questionable as few boatmen could read. It is known, however, that they were enforced. In 1868 a newspaper reported fines being imposed on two consecutive days on boatmen entering the tunnel after they had been told to wait for other boats to come out. The tunnel has had various lengths in its 200-plus years' existence. It began at 2,966 yards, but then was extended to 3,063 yards in 1890 at its western end, for the railway from Butterley to Ripley. In 1976, it was extended by a further 20 yards for the A38 dual carriageway.

When the 1964 expedition members went into the tunnel, high water made for an easy passage – until they reached some of the roof supports, around which they had to negotiate their boat in the dark. (David Dawson)

In contrast, when Robin Witter explored the tunnel by canoe in October 1979, the A38 had been built over the western end, the stop planks removed, and the water level was considerably lower. About 100 yards in, he noted that the rail-supported arch of the 1890 extension changed to the original bore which had wooden supports. One wonders if the extension was built with supports in place, knowing that the tunnel was already subsiding (it was closed from 1889 to 1894 whilst a collapse further along was repaired). (RW)

About 600 yards into the tunnel, the feed from Butterley Reservoir, which is directly above, came down a vertical shaft into a side tunnel. Viewed from the main tunnel, a cascade of water can be seen at the end of the 20-yard-long adit. There is timber reinforcing at regular intervals across the width of the adit. At this time (1979) the water entering the main tunnel was flowing westwards. The stop planks at the western portal, which had forced the water to flow eastwards, were no longer in place. This was presumably because there was no longer any need to supply water to Codnor Park Forge which had closed in 1965. (RW)

After exactly 40 chains (880 yards), directly beneath the Butterley Company works, the tunnel widens out to 15ft so that boats could be moored for loading or unloading without impeding through traffic. Vertical shafts enabled the goods to be hoisted up to, or lowered down from the works. This view shows the western end of the 'Wide Hole' where the tunnel reverts to its normal 9ft bore. Note the large corner stones, no doubt to offer strength against impact from boats. (RW)

Various tunnels led off from the Wide Hole. Heading east, the first on the right, seen here, was the largest and gave access to a 9ft diameter vertical shaft from Butterley works. Goods were presumably transferred from the base of the shaft to the boat which would have been tied adjacent to the opening seen here. (RW)

A little further along the Wide Hole a second access to the same shaft, seen here on the right, was bricked up in 1915. Ahead, the Wide Hole was narrowed in the same year over a length of 45ft, where the tunnel arch passed directly beneath two further shafts from Butterley Works. Boat access was deliberately and expensively maintained by the construction of the smaller arch. A small length of the Wide Hole beyond the narrowing was left unaltered before the tunnel reverted to its 9ft bore. (RW)

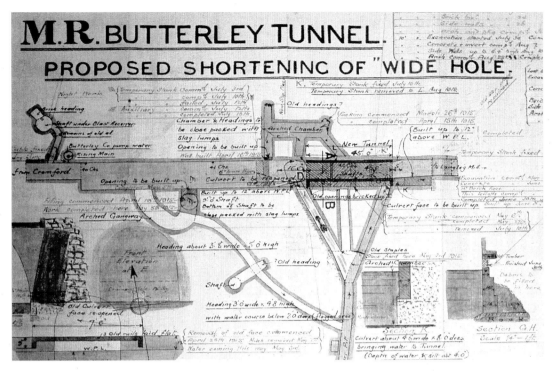

A plan and cross-sections of the proposed shortening of the Wide Hole showing some of the adjacent shafts and adits. Although not decipherable at this scale, details of exactly when each bit of work was carried out, mainly in 1915, are noted on the plan.

Beyond the Wide Hole, Robin Witter had to abandon his canoe, and walk on the loose stones covering the twin pipes, laid in the 1920s to maintain the water supply from Butterley Reservoir to Codnor Park forge. At 1,100 yards from the western portal he found these collapsed supporting timbers and decided not to risk going any further. However, he noted that he could not see any light from the vertical ventilation shaft known to be 200 yards further on, so assumed the tunnel was completely blocked before the shaft. (RW)

Left: With no towpath through the tunnel, horses had to be led over the top. At Double Bridge, the horse path passed under two railways, each with their well-built stone bridges. The lower bridge carried a branch of the Butterley Company's private railway from their works to Hartshay Colliery. The upper one took the branch of the Midland Railway from Ripley to Pentrich Junction on the Pye Bridge–Ambergate line, the same line that caused the initial lengthening of Butterley Tunnel around 1890.

Below: Looking west, we see canvas trunking, no doubt connected to a pump bringing fresh air into the workings (the tunnel was blocked at this time so there would be no through air flow, apart from via an occasional ventilation shaft). The wooden box on the left seems to be suspended from above by chains, suggesting they are at the base of such a shaft. The wooden decking has been put in slightly above normal water level. The brick arch is supported by steel rails with timber packing. *(LK)*

Butterley Tunnel (looking from Cromford) 22·6·1909.

Although we do not know where in the tunnel this work was taking place, the caption tells us that it was on 22 June 1909. The tunnel by now had little chance of being reopened, but maintenance and repair work continued at least until the 1920s when pipes were laid in the bed to ensure a continued water supply to Codnor Park Forge, which the railway company, as owners of the canal, were legally obliged to supply. The work seen here is probably concerned with maintaining or reinstating that water supply.

Looking east, we appear to be beneath the decking seen in the previous photograph, with evidence of fresh rock falls at this level that would normally be full of water. The shadowy figures of at least six men can be made out in the distance. Perhaps mining subsidence had caused the tunnel floor to collapse, but left the roof intact. (LK)

Above: The Ambergate to Pye Bridge branch railway originally crossed Butterley Reservoir on this trestle viaduct, seen here around 1910. Some fifteen years later it was replaced by the present causeway which still carries steam trains today as part of the Midland Railway Centre's operations. (Wilf Marshall)

Left: In 1968, Butterley Reservoir was under the control of British Waterways Board, as it remains today. (HD)

Above the eastern end of the tunnel was the much smaller Butterley Park reservoir, which was drained in the 1930s to save on future maintenance. The outlet leading to the eastern end of Butterley Tunnel is seen in the foreground on 22 June 1909. (LK)

Although the eastern portal of Butterley Tunnel was gated, it was not always locked! When the water level was low, access was possible, although the mud could be treacherous. In 1979, the higher outside water level was held back by stop planks offering this unusual view. (RW)

The only known photograph of a boat making a through passage of the tunnel is of de Salis's Fellows Morton & Clayton horse boat *Tipton* in 1897, seen here leaving the eastern portal on its return from Cromford to the main canal system. (Hugh McKnight)

The railway photographer was busy on 22 June 1909, as he also took this image of the new concrete spillway from Butterley Park Reservoir feeding the canal at the eastern portal of Butterley Tunnel. In the tunnel mouth is one of the distinctive maintenance boats used on this canal. Above it is the height gauge and by now redundant sign with tunnel entry hours. The wooden gate to the left of the boat was presumably to close off the entrance. (LK)

When Butterley Park Reservoir was drained, its bank was breached and this new spillway was installed to carry away water still draining into it. The Golden Valley Light Railway has since been built across the bed of the reservoir and the top of this spillway, before continuing on the embankment to the right as far as the Newlands Inn. In June 1969, the canal was well silted up and the tunnel portal was only half visible. A crude wooden barricade prevented water running back into the tunnel, prior to the steel gate being fitted. (HD)

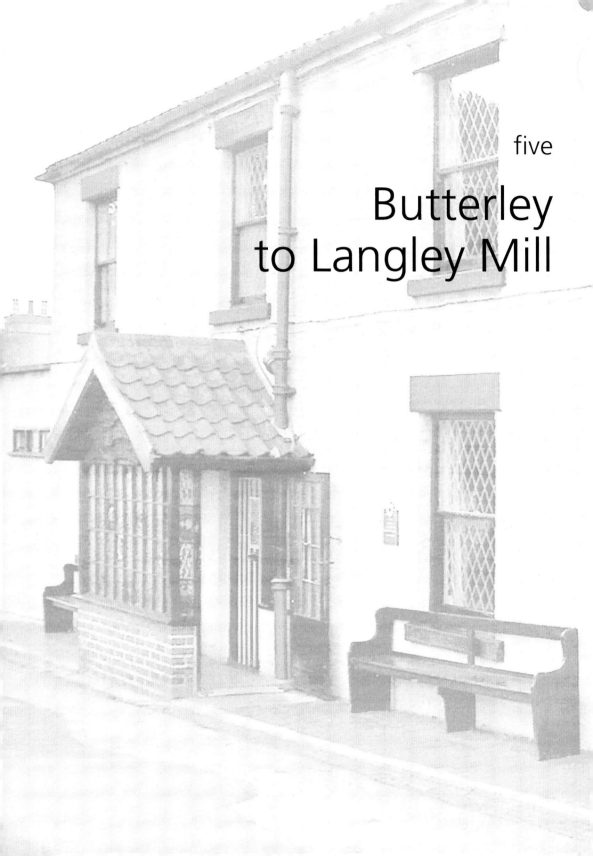

five

Butterley
to Langley Mill

The culverting of the bridge (no. 34) at Golden Valley has begun in this June 1973 view. The road was previously known as Greenhill Lane. The Newlands Inn had developed from a farm house built around 1760. Today there is little sign of the canal here – just a grassy slope with two concrete pipes to carry any remaining water. The distinctive brickwork around the arch was added to strengthen the original arch, which can be just made out above it. The original bridge is seen below, with temporary wooden struts prior to rebuilding. (HD)

This view of the original Bridge 34 at Golden Valley shows the timber supports under the already rather flat arch of the bridge prior to the more permanent brick strengthening. To the right of the bridge stands what was then the Co-op shop, believed to have had deliveries by canal. Three men are busy around the chickens in the right foreground, but it is not clear what they are doing. The small brick building behind them is no longer there. To the left behind the bridge is the steeple of St Mathias' church, later used as a school. Bricks for its construction are said to have been delivered from Buckland Hollow by canal in 1876. (Doris Ball)

This wooden bridge once gave access from the cottages at Golden Valley across the canal to the Coach Road, on the far side of which were allotments. It also carried a mains water pipe. Numbered 35, it was replaced around 1948 by the iron-sided bridge which still stands, although it was closed off in 2002 as the decking was unsafe. (Doris Ball)

The view from Bridge 35 on 25 March 1981 when the canal had been dredged and neat wooden piling installed as part of improvements to Golden Valley. The restored stone cottages won an architectural award. These are the same cottages as seen on page 6, but the warehouse, which once stood at the far end, has long been demolished.

CODNOR PARK
MONUMENT.

BRITISH WATERWAYS
CODNOR PARK
RESERVOIR
(CAPACITY 33,000,000 GALLONS)
ALL ENQUIRIES TO
THE DIVISIONAL MANAGER
BRITISH WATERWAYS
NORTH EASTERN DIVISION
P.O. BOX 9 NO. 1 DOCK STREET
LEEDS 1

Above: On the hill to the south is the Jessop Monument, completed in 1858 by public subscription from Butterley workers as a memorial to William Jessop II, who died in 1852. He developed the company after the death of his father, the canal engineer and Butterley Company partner. Despite being damaged by lightning strike in 1861, it was a popular place for festivities, and this scene is thought to be on Whit Monday 1908. (Peter Ludlam)

Left: Codnor Park Reservoir was built immediately alongside the canal in the angle formed by the main line and its Pinxton Branch, which passes just in front of the houses of Ironville, seen at the end of the reservoir. (IM)

Opposite below: This fine figure of a lock keeper is standing by the top of the Ironville flight of locks in 1897 awaiting the arrival of de Salis's boat, which we first saw at Cromford (page 14). Note the very crude balance beam, scarcely more than a tree trunk. In the background is No 1 Monument Lane and, to the left, the Mechanics Institute. (Hugh McKnight)

CODNOR PARK, RIPLEY.

Above: At the end of Codnor Park Reservoir, the Pinxton branch left under this stone bridge. The main line continued to the right, immediately entering the first lock just to the right of the bollard. The water in the foreground is the entrance to a private level branch canal, built by the Butterley Company to the top of their lime kilns close to Lock 6. Much of its route later became a railway; the remaining short length gave access to a boat dock by Lock 2. (BK)

On 9 September 1984 British Waterways were removing the top lock as part of the work deemed necessary under the then new Reservoir Act. Opinion today is that this work, which effectively destroyed the amenity value of the canal in Ironville, was grossly in excess of that required. The Pinxton Branch junction bridge in the background is all that survives today. (Mike Haddon)

By June 1985 work had progressed and all traces of the historic top lock had been removed. The channel was lined with special matting to help carry away the vast flow of water that would result should the reservoir ever seriously overtop. It never has. (Kevin Lane)

The view from Cinder Bank, Ironville, in 1952 where it crosses the canal above Boat Dock Lock 2. Although the canal had been closed for eight years, the locks were still intact. The prominent wall, now merely a grass slope, was made largely from iron furnace slag. The boat dock was to the left, between canal and road; traces can still be seen. A canal company carpenter's shop once stood on the right, half way between the two locks. Today, the chamber of Lock 2 survives, as does the junction bridge in the background. (Fred Copeland)

The toll gate beside Cinder Bank Bridge (36) at Ironville on the Coach Road, a private road owned by the Butterley Company. Although the gate and sign are long gone, one of the stone posts was still in place in 2003 with the woodwork of the gate attached. The Butterley Company railway was on the left and the then shortened canal arm originating by the top lock ran on its contour as far as the boat dock to the right, just above Lock 2.

On the offside between locks 2 and 3 stands 'The Pottery', seen here on 30 August 1971. It was the remaining building of the small earthenware pottery begun in the 1820s by Butterley employee William Burton, and sold in 1846 to Joseph Bourne of Denby. Beyond is a now demolished terrace of cottages, with the roof of the Mechanics Institute beyond them.

In 1981, water flowed freely over the concrete weir that replaced the top gates of Lock 4. Sadly the reservoir work (see page 82) necessitated the removal of these weirs, reducing the open water to a mere trickle in a reed and rubbish infested canal bed. To the right are the original canal stables, later used for horses belonging to Codnor Park & Ironville Co-op. It was known locally as 'The Mortuary', as it was where suicides and accidental deaths from the canal and reservoir were laid out. To the left is the Butterley Company's Mechanics Institute, built in 1846, comprising library, lecture hall and coffee room. It was later used as offices for the Butterley Company's colliery and is now converted into apartments.

Below Lock 5 stood the canal company's house and workshops, built after 1811 and seen here between 1875 – when the Jacksdale railway viaduct (seen in the background) was opened – and 1910 – when the house extension was built to add a kitchen and extra bedroom. There was no proper road access to the house, so deliveries of coal etc were made to the opposite bank and carried across the canal on the small boat tied just outside the cottage. The lower storey of the workshops to the right housed a saw pit for building lock gates. (Steve Footitt)

The Jacksdale School Outing of 1970/71 with the retired canal inspector, ninety-year-old Charles Gibson, who lived in the house below Lock 5. He began work as a bricklayer and worked his way up to inspector and was one of the last people to leg through Butterley Tunnel. He kept gardens which were the talk of the neighbourhood, and frequently featured in the local press. (Denise Scotese, Jacksdale Heritage)

The canal inspector's house below Lock 5 in the early 1970s, when Charles Gibson still lived there. Beyond it are the workshops and a small office. On the right are the roofs of the now demolished Limekiln Row, formerly called Measham Row, beside Lock 6. (JP)

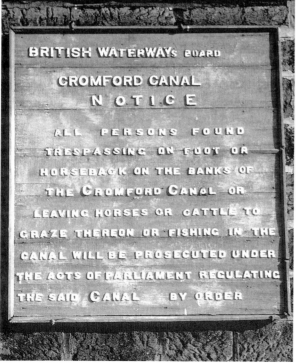

BRITISH WATERWAYS BOARD

CROMFORD CANAL
N O T I C E

ALL PERSONS FOUND
TRESPASSING ON FOOT OR
HORSEBACK ON THE BANKS OF
THE CROMFORD CANAL OR
LEAVING HORSES OR CATTLE TO
GRAZE THEREON OR FISHING IN THE
CANAL WILL BE PROSECUTED UNDER
THE ACTS OF PARLIAMENT REGULATING
THE SAID CANAL   BY ORDER

Above: Looking up the Ironville or Codnor Park flight of locks towards the canal company house and office, with the last outhouse of Limekiln Row on the left. In the foreground are the unpainted but intact gates of Lock 6, apparently with a spike placed in the ground to stop them opening. (JP)

Left: On the side of the small office building, seen by the fence in the photograph above, was this 'official' sign composed of individual white letters attached to a blue-painted wooden board. It is still intact and in safe storage the Pump House at Langley Mill. (HD)

Above: The canal company buildings above Lock 6 on 30 August 1971. The larger of the buildings on the right was the workshop, including a forge and saw pit. Rings in the wall suggested horses were tied here whilst being re-shoed. To the left of that is the small 'office'. In the foreground can be seen the stop plank grooves at the head of a shallow dry dock. This was built after 1911, although its lack of depth indicates that it was intended for horse boats only.

Right: The last boat ever to use the dock was this wooden ice-breaker, seen here being inspected by pupils of Wigan Grammar School in March 1963 who had been brought on a field visit by their young and enthusiastic teacher Ian Moss, who still lectured on canals in the North West forty years later. The boat was probably one that had been used on maintenance duties before the canal's closure and bore the letters LMS on the bows. (IM)

Looking down the flight with the top gates of Lock 6 on the left and the dry dock entry to their right. To the right of that, the remaining house of Limekiln Row, with the chimneys of Butterley Company's Codnor Park Forge beyond. This and the photograph below were taken at Whitsun 1960. (TWT/W)

The tail gates of Lock 6 stand open with the buildings of Codnor Park forge alongside the canal pound leading to Lock 7. Close examination of the original photograph reveals a cast metal figure 6 on the balance beam between the two uprights. (TWT/W)

In 1968, all that remained of the Codnor Park forge was the gable end wall, which stood dramatically alongside the weedy canal bed in this view up towards locks 7 and 6. In 2002-03, the whole of the forge site was opencast for coal which involved temporarily infilling part of Lock 7 for an access road and creating a wholly alien landscape of hills and deep holes on the previously level site. (HD)

The bridge across the main canal to the left, below the Ironville flight, was a Butterley 'Standard' Bridge, installed on 27 November 1943. It was an example of one which could be built in different widths and lengths for wartime, from five basic parts. It was demolished in 1998. By 1835 the original stone Lawn Bridge on this site had been rebuilt to carry the tramway from collieries at Kirkby and Selston into Codnor Park Works. This involved the construction of the raised causeway across the flood plain of the Erewash, to the right, which can still be seen today. The tramway bridge was demolished in 1903. To the right is the towpath bridge across the entrance to Portland Basin, part of which is seen in the next photograph. (BK)

From Jacksdale Station, high on its Great Northern Railway viaduct demolished in 1974, are seen the remains of Portland Basin. It was built in 1822 as a terminus for the 3-mile tramway, including two rope-worked inclined planes, from Butterley Company's Portland Colliery at Selston. Boats accessed the large basin over a cast iron aqueduct, now removed, across the infant River Erewash immediately after the towpath bridge of the previous photograph. On the left is Stone Row, Jacksdale's first housing, also now gone. (JP)

A railway level view of the demolition of what was locally known as 'Black Bridge' (no. 39) just north of Lock 8. Opened in 1876, the branch linked the Great Northern Railway to Codnor Park Works, later to the Midland Railway, and closed in 1954. The brick pillar from which this view was taken in the late 1960s still stands close to where the water that now trickles down the Ironville Lock flight finally leaves the canal for the River Erewash. South of here the canal bed is infilled. (Eddie Wilbraham)

For some reason, perhaps because of their relative isolation, the locks at Stoneyford were rarely photographed. This is one of a series of photographs taken in 1907 of every set of top and bottom gates on the canal, possibly connected with the enquiry into the abandonment of Butterley Tunnel. This is Stoneyford Lock 9 with gates in good order. (IA)

The Boat Inn at Stoneyford is isolated on today's road system, but was no doubt welcomed by boatmen in the past. It has been smartened up from its August 1972 appearance and is now The Stoneyford Lodge – a pub, restaurant, motel and private night club. (TWT/W)

This cottage at Stoneyford, by what was originally called Hunt's Bridge, may have pre-dated the canal. A lock keeper's cottage was more likely to have been built beside one of the three locks. Mr and Mrs Black lived here for many years, the former working at Codnor Park Forge, the latter at The Boat Inn, just up Boat Lane to the right. The ice was obviously thick enough to take a person's weight even so near the bridge. (HD)

The cottage is one of the few features still recognisable on the canal's route in the Stoneyford area today. There was no sign of canal nor bridge by the 1970s. More recently the building was part of a boarding kennels. This area was opencast and backfilled, so traces of the canal are very hard to find, although a footpath roughly follows its course. (JP)

The shortest pound on the canal was between Stoneyford Deep and Shallow locks, nos 10 and 11, seen here in 1907. The houses to the left were Dovecote Row, and to the right are Erewash Cottages where Boat Lane ended. Very little of the habitation between here and Langley Mill survived the opencasting of the 1960s. (IA)

The village of Stoneyford lay above Bentley (or Benty) Bridge (42), but there is virtually nothing to be seen today, apart from Stoneyford Lodge to the left. The bridge was formerly called Roystone Bridge, and lay just below Shallow Lock 11. The remains of the embankment leading to the railway bridge, that once crossed the canal in front of this bridge, can still be made out in the photograph on both sides of the canal. (Stuart Byfield)

A couple pose beside Bentley, or Benty, Bridge (no. 42) with the gates of Stoneyford Shallow Lock visible through the arch. In those days, the canal was obviously the place to be seen! The bridge is unusual for two reasons: it is built of brick instead of stone, and it has no proper towpath under it. The towpath in fact changed sides at this bridge, in anticipation of the canal crossing the River Erewash between here and the next lock. (HD)

When the aqueduct (of which no photographs are known) over the River Erewash was demolished, it was replaced by this footbridge. Remains of the brickwork of the abutments for the aqueduct arch can still be seen by the bridge when the water level is sufficiently low. The skyline today has changed from this 1968 scene in which the opencast work that destroyed the canal dominates the background. (HD)

Between the aqueduct and Vicker's Lock 12 stood Wharf Row, Brinsley. As happened at Stoneyford, these houses were demolished and the area was subsequently opencast for coal. Notice the ample width of the canal where today there are just fields. In the foreground is the ground paddle gear for the lock. (Stuart Byfield)

Vicker's or Limekiln Lock 12 in 1907. To the right, above and below the lock, lay Clinton Wharf, served by a railway from the nearby colliery. The small square hole in the right-hand lock wall may have been the outlet for a by-wash, which allowed excess water to pass down the canal. However, Jessop's canals normally relied on this water passing through the ground paddle sluices beside the top gates and running over the bottom gates, which would be built slightly lower than the top gates, as on the Ironville flight. (IA)

All but the last half mile of canal had officially been abandoned in 1944, but until opencasting began little was done with it. In 1954, Inland Waterways Association committee members Mr C.F. Clements and Pat Saunders, on Pat's boat *Mistress Mine,* navigated the Erewash Canal and attempted to continue up the Cromford. The top ground paddles of Lock 14 were completely choked and the lock had to be filled from leaks in the top gates. It took over 5 hours to pass through. To try and make them watertight, the bottom gates were caulked, a tarpaulin was tacked over the gates, ashes sifted down and newspaper and puddle used to stop leaks. Finally a team of some twenty adults and children 'sprung' the top gates against a 10-inch difference in water level. (TWT/A)

Above the lock they came across two sunken boats in the channel. These are in fact the same two boats pictured in a rather less decayed state on page 99. *Mistress Mine* just managed to squeeze by. The bridges below Lock 13 can be seen ahead. (TWT/A)

Right: The bottom gates of Lock 13 could not be opened beyond this point despite prolonged efforts, so this is as far as *Mistress Mine* managed to navigate. In true pioneering fashion, however, they did run a 'boat trip' between locks 13 and 14, some hundreds of yards, carrying part of the crowd which had gathered. *Mistress Mine* was almost certainly the last boat to navigate this length of the Cromford Canal. Even when restoration takes place, the exact route will not be followed here as the A610 road embankment has obliterated this section, and a diversion will be necessary. (TWT/A)

Below: Lock 13 still looked to be in a good state of repair in 1962 when John Wain took this family photograph. Proving that canals can get into the blood, his sons (Simon on the left and Rex on the right) are now well-respected boat builders! The construction of the A610 road has completely changed the scene beyond the lock where it now crosses on a massive embankment. (John Wain)

Lock 13, known as Strutt's, Marshall's or Tommy's Lock, seen from Marshall's Bridge (46) which crossed immediately below it. Locks and bridges often took their name from local landowners and an 1811 map names this Day's Bridge after John Day who owned the land on both sides. By 31 August 1963 vandalism was beginning to take its toll on the unused canal and all but one of the balance beams had been broken off. (IM)

Marshall's Lock 13 and road bridge from below, with the Barber Walker colliery railway bridge adjacent. The railway bridge survived in use until Moorgreen Colliery closed in 1985 – long after the lock had been demolished and the canal infilled. (MG)

Two gas tar narrowboats – motor *Mayflower* and butty *Excellent* – sunk below Lock 13 where they were abandoned after traffic ceased, some time in the early 1940s. Both boats belonged to Kempson & Company who owned the 'acid works' at Pye Bridge. They were built by Rudkins of Leicester in 1926 and 1921, respectively, and were almost certainly the last boats to trade above Beggarlee Wharf. (IA)

Half-way between locks 13 and 14 lay Beggarlee Wharf, where coal was delivered from local pits by railway wagons from which it was tipped onto the conveyor in the centre of the photograph to be loaded into narrowboats. The coal came in a continuous stream, so the men here are slowly pushing the boat along to ensure an even load. Whilst the rest of the canal was closed in 1944, this last half mile carried regular traffic until 1952. (Hugh Cauldwell)

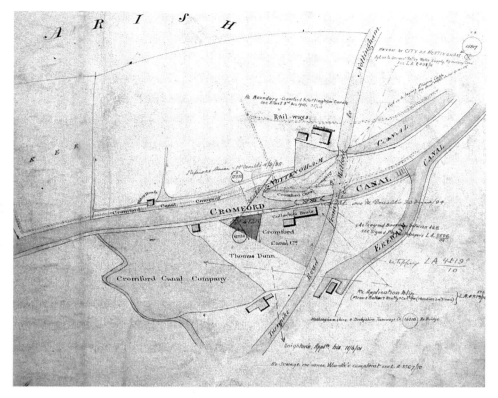

The layout of the watercourses around the junction of the three canals at Langley Mill was, and still is, complex. This map of 1811 (north is to the left) gives an idea of how the Cromford Canal joined the later Nottingham Canal by a stop lock (to prevent loss of water to the newcomer) above Lock 14, and the Erewash Canal just below the lock. A stop lock was not needed here, as the Erewash Company would have insisted on all water that came down the Cromford entering their canal. Having reached Langley Mill before the Nottingham Canal, the Cromford Canal Company had taken the opportunity to buy most of the land immediately north of the Matlock–Nottingham turnpike road. At the terminus of the Erewash Canal there were two basins, with a dry dock in between, and it is here that the feed water enters that canal.

On 31 August 1963, just after the last half mile of the Cromford Canal was officially abandoned, the elegant yellow-on-blue lettering of the sign at Langley Mill still proclaimed it to be the junction of the three canals. Today, such hand-crafted lettering is simply not seen on any official signs on our waterways. (IM)

Early in the twentieth century, a boatwoman poses with her horse at Langley Mill. Whilst the boats on short-haul traffics would have been crewed by men who returned home each evening, or slept on board for only an occasional night, the longer-distance traffics were carried on boats where the whole family lived aboard permanently and helped out with the daily tasks. (Hugh Cauldwell)

Langley Bridge Lock 14 in the early 1960s, with planks removed from the top gates to drain the pound prior to infilling. The Cromford Canal Company's toll house is on the left, from where passing boats were 'gauged' to ascertain the weight of cargo carried, and hence the tolls to be paid. The extant Nottingham Canal toll house is on the right. (MG)

The lock cottage and toll house beside the gateless Lock 14 at Langley Mill, still in apparently good condition. Although today such a canalside property would fetch a fortune, in 1963 canals were still thought of as liabilities not assets, so British Waterways bulldozed the cottage into the lock chamber. Permit books that recorded the passage of boats were stored in the building and fortunately some were rescued from a bonfire and donated to the Derbyshire Record Office. The chimney of Vic Hallam's works can just be seen in the left background. (MG)

The boat crews have gathered at Langley Mill during a boatmen's strike, probably that of employees of Fellows Morton & Clayton, which lasted from 13 August to 19 November 1923 and brought traffic to a virtual standstill all over the canal network. The sheer-legs are over the Nottingham Canal stop lock and to the right is the Great Northern Inn. (MG)

Langley Bridge Lock, the last on the Cromford Canal, in 1907, looking more like a working lock should. Although Butterley Tunnel had been closed since 1900, traffic continued on the southern section up until 1952. However, the scene is obviously much quieter than it was during the strike of 1923, when boaters gathered together. There is a single empty boat above the lock, and the crew appear to be posing for the photographer. (IA)

Two unladen horse boats lie on the Cromford Canal at Langley Mill in 1921, just above the Nottingham Canal stop lock, where sheer legs are placed over each set of gates. (John Hobbs)

These sheer legs appear in several photographs of Langley Mill, so must have been in place for some years. They are technically not on the Cromford Canal but over the two sets of gates on the stop lock of the Nottingham Canal, which joined it here. Normally they would have been used to lift the gates out for repair or replacement, but here they appear to be holding a large board which might be used instead of the more conventional stop planks to seal off a section of canal for maintenance. There is a winch to the left, weighted down with large stones and supporting the stop board. (MG)

The very end of the Cromford Canal runs seamlessly into the Erewash Canal, whose terminal basins are along the arm to the left. Two empty narrowboats wait to go up Langley Bridge Lock, out of which is approaching an Upper Trent wide boat. As no horse is visible, it may well be a motor boat, but in any case it is not obvious how a horse would get across the entrance to the Erewash basin without a long detour. (Hugh Cauldwell)

six

Leawood Arm

One of the last boats to carry cargo on the canal west of Butterley Tunnel lies sunk and decaying in the Leawood Arm, close to its junction with the main line, in about 1940. The stonework of Wigwell Aqueduct can be seen to the right of the two figures. This short arm was built between 1800 and 1802 by Peter Nightingale, great uncle of the more famous Florence, to serve his cotton mills and lead smelters. Lead was carried by boat the short distance from Lea Wharf to the Cromford & High Peak Railway well into the twentieth century, whilst coal was delivered to Lea Mills from Hartshay up until the 1930s.

When the Manchester, Buxton, Matlock & Midlands Junction Railway came northwards from Ambergate in the 1840s, it first had to pass under the main line of the canal, then through the 315-yard Leawood Tunnel and under the Leawood Arm. To do this the railway company installed an iron trough, as at all other railway aqueducts on this canal, but faced it with elegant stonework, something they omitted for the nearby crossing under the canal's main line. Perhaps this was at the insistence of Peter Nightingale. By the 1880s, the original bridge across the river (above right) was life-expired, and the railway took the opportunity to rebuild the bridge and also realign the track between here and the far side of Leawood Pump, bringing the railway much closer to the canal and, in the process, causing the demolition of the Junction Inn. Taken in 1888 by the railway to show progress on the bridge reconstruction, this is the only known photograph to clearly show the aqueduct, whose iron trough can be seen beneath the curving stonework. The aqueduct was taken down, probably in the late 1940s or early 1950s, and replaced by the present footbridge. (Bill Hudson)

Although this 1888 photograph was taken to show the old railway bridge across the Derwent at Leawood, immediately prior to its replacement by the one seen on the opposite page, the aqueduct carrying the Leawood Arm can be glimpsed to the right. (Bill Hudson)

At the end of the arm stood Lea Wharf, although until 1819 the arm had continued all the way to Lea Mills. A complicated dispute over water rights caused Nightingale to go to the expense of truncating the arm and moving the wharf and weighing machine here. Piles of what may be coal lie on the wharf towards the end of its commercial life in the 1930s, whilst two men work to transfer cargo between the rather down-at-heel boat and a cart. In front of them is a neat stack of lead ingots which would be loaded here for the short run to the Cromford & High Peak Railway for onward transport. A second narrowboat lies up the narrow basin beyond. The base of the crane can still be seen on the wharf today. (George Wigglesworth)

On 21 April 1905, William Henry Stockwell took this photograph of Lea Wharf. It is piled high with huge lumps of coal. A second large stack, of what looks like stone, lies to the right beside a large 'Scotch' derrick partly hidden by the trees. A single empty boat waits at the wharf, where the crane is almost invisible behind a stack of what are probably lead ingots. Beyond the wharf lay the former hat factory, which ceased operation in the 1870s and was later used as a wool warehouse and mineral water plant. It finally collapsed in 1955. (Julie Simpson)

Traffic to and from Lea Wharf finished around 1936. In January 1969 the original wharfinger's house had just been extended over the site of the weighing machine to make the attractive residence that it remains today. (HD)

seven

Pinxton Branch

The Pinxton Arm was always an integral part of the Cromford Canal. In fact Pinxton was linked to the national canal system before Cromford, because of delays on Butterley Tunnel and Wigwell Aqueduct. The collieries along its length also had the advantage that wide boats carrying up to 50 tons could be used, instead of narrowboats with half that capacity. In this distant view of Ironville, the brickworks are prominent in the foreground. Just to the left of them is the bridge carrying the main line towpath across the Pinxton Arm, beyond which the arm runs along the eastern dam wall of Codnor Park Reservoir before curving right under the flat decked Butterley Company Bridge (2). The bridges on the arm were numbered separately.

Church Bridge (3) at Ironville was a popular subject for postcards, probably because it was, by the beginning of the twentieth century, one of the few picturesque scenes in the town. Ironville was built by the Butterley Company for its workers as a model village, but standards declined over the years, and in the 1960s, rather than upgrade the historic rows of terraces, many were demolished. The church, funded by the Butterley Company, stands to the left. Its cemetery lies opposite, across the canal, which is now infilled and the bridge removed. (BK)

The Midland Railway crossed the Pinxton Arm on this two-arched bridge, the right-hand arch accommodating a road to a farm and the Old House at Home, a somewhat isolated canalside pub. On 20 August 1956, ex LMS Beyer-Garratt loco 47979 is held at Pye Bridge Junction signals. Today, the bridge still stands, but the land beyond has been completely destroyed by the Smotherfly opencast workings. (Peter Stevenson)

In the days before the internal combustion engine there were only two ways to clear a canal – by steam dredger or, as here in 1907 near Pinxton, by a 'spoon dredger'. Two men operated a primitive crane on the end of which was a large ladle which the third man manoeuvred to 'spoon' out the mud and deposit it into the boat. This apparently primitive technique was used well into the twentieth century. (TWT/B)

Whilst the Old House at Home was demolished in the 1960s, a canalside pub that does still exist, largely unchanged, is the Boat Inn at Pinxton. Seen here probably in the 1950s, the canal was well overgrown after some ten years' disuse. This section was restored in the 1980s and is now an attractive, but isolated, length of canal. (Alf Henshaw/J.R. Bonser)

Another primitive technique for clearing out a canal is seen here at the terminal basin at Pinxton Wharf where workers are standing on planks laid across the reed beds and digging them out with spades. The picture is tentatively dated 1906 but it is a very different scene from the pre–1910 scene below. (TWT/M)

Pinxton nos 1 and 6 pits, plus the then new workshops and generator house, are shown in this postcard franked in 1910. The girls, only just visible in this card, are Clara and Hilda Watson and Maggie Garratt from Meadow Rows, which were just to the right. It was taken from some way down the canal by the 'wharf' where an arm goes off to the north. The house at the end can be recognised from the photograph above, suggesting that just the end of the canal had become weeded up through disuse. The final section of the canal was restored by Derbyshire County Council in 1983–84 to form a fishing and amenity area. (Peter Ludlam)

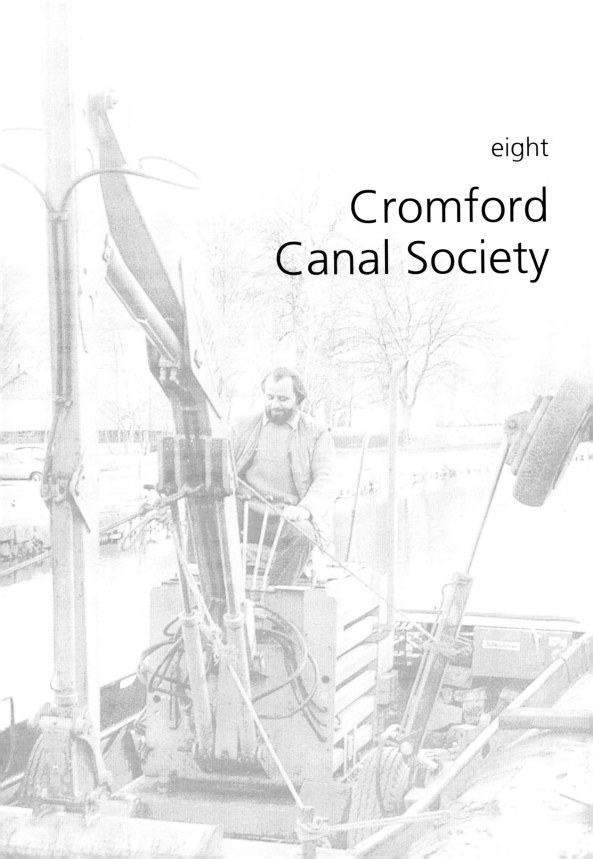

eight

Cromford Canal Society

The Cromford Canal Society's *John Gray* unloading passengers at Cromford on 29 July 1978. Formed in 1972, the Society began work in earnest on restoration of the canal after it had been transferred from British Waterways to Derbyshire County Council. By July 1977 dredging had reached Leawood from Cromford. This enabled the horse-drawn boat *John Gray*, specially built for CCS, to offer public trips at weekends and charter trips during the week. Such was the popularity of the service that, in 1982, over 15,000 passengers were carried between Cromford and Leawood, about half on charter trips (including many school groups) and half on public trips.

Dredging the long-neglected bed of the canal in 1974. With restricted access, the excavator had to be driven across the field from the nearby A6 to begin work here, just north of Lawn Bridge (1). This dredging, and the subsequent regular passage of *John Gray* for many seasons, kept the canal clear for thirty years, but gradual siltation means that it will soon need re-dredging if its attractive appearance and value as a wildlife habitat is to be maintained. (SS)

On 3 May 1980, the canal and Leawood Pumphouse were formally reopened by the Duke of Devonshire, President of the Cromford Canal Society. As he cuts the ribbon from the bows of *John Gray*, he is closely watched by CCS founder and chairman Dr Desmond Stoker. (SS)

Offering a scheduled service on Saturdays and Sundays, the horse boat *John Gray* was always popular with trippers and walkers alike. The boat was named after a Sheffield surgeon who, in his spare time, was the guiding light behind the restoration of Leawood Pump House.

In early 1984, the society acquired this unusual floating dredger, comprising a Smalley Long Reach Excavator mounted on a work punt fitted with independent hydraulic stabilisers. Canal Manager Simon Stoker is at the controls.

The canal became a prestigious place to be seen. On 29 April 1986 it was used for a pre by-election publicity trip by West Derbyshire Conservatives. MP Patrick McLoughlin is posing for the press on the gunwale of *John Gray* at Cromford Wharf. (SS)

The Cromford Canal featured, albeit briefly, in the filming of a television adaptation of George Eliot's novel *Silas Marner*. It starred Ben Kingsley, Jenny Agutter, and the nationally less well-known Simon Stoker (right) and Dennis Shooter. They appeared, with *John Gray* well disguised, plus boat horse Major, for all of 8 seconds after the day's filming on 29 March 1985. (SS)

The *John Gray's* success caused it to be lengthened twice to increase capacity. Built in 1977 by West Riding Boat Company, it was originally 36ft long. First lengthened in 1979, in 1982 it had a further section added in the centre, bringing it up to 60ft. Because of its length, it returned with a police escort and had great difficulty making the turn into Cromford Meadows. Direct access from the road to the wharf was out of the question! It was then craned back into the water.

The swing bridge across the main canal at the southern end of the aqueduct, by the junction with the Leawood Arm, was rebuilt in 1988 by canal manager Simon Stoker and his Job Creation team. It was modelled on a photograph of the original bridge, which had been built to enable horses to transfer from the northern to southern bank as the towpath changes sides here. When canals were built into hillsides, towpaths were always built on the side away from the hill so that the maximum width of embankment supported the water in the canal. A second example of such a swing bridge was once to be seen on the aqueduct at Bullbridge where the canal crossed the River Amber. (SS)

With *John Gray* operating regularly to Leawood, restoration continued southwards using a specially modified pontoon-mounted Smalley 5T dredger. In 1987 it is seen working towards the railway aqueduct in an almost drained canal just south of Wigwell Aqueduct. (SS)

The Smalley dredger was specially designed to fit through the bridges and is seen here in May 1988 emerging from the southern portal of Gregory Tunnel. (SS)

On 13 August 1988, founder and chairman of the Cromford Canal Society Dr Desmond Stoker undertook a sponsored bow haul of *John Gray* to celebrate his eightieth year. He succeeded in pulling the boat all the way from Leawood to Cromford and is seen here at the swing bridge by High Peak Junction workshops. (SS)

The Cromford Canal Society dredged the whole of the DCC-owned length of canal to its terminus at Ambergate. On the southern section a land-based dredger was used. Its limited reach allowed clearance of silt only to roughly half way across the channel. Simon Stoker is negotiating Gratton's Bridge (15) with the aid of steel beams across the canal, as the towpath beneath the bridge was too narrow for the tracks. Since completion of the dredging, the canal south of Leawood has almost completely silted up once again, preventing water flow and inhibiting wildlife. (SS)

By late 1988, dredging of the canal from Leawood to Gregory Wide Hole, at the south end of the Gregory Tunnel, was complete. On 21 December 1988 *John Gray* made a special trip for the members of the Job Creation Scheme who had worked on the project and is seen pausing at the northern portal of Gregory Tunnel. (SS)

Continuing on its return to Leawood, *John Gray*, towed by the paddle-powered work punt, crosses the railway aqueduct. Sadly, this was to be the only boat trip made on this section of canal. On 25 February 1989, after severe storms and melting snow had blocked run-offs, the canal overtopped its bank between Leawood and Gregory Tunnel and eroded the embankment (see page 30), causing the canal water level to be lowered, never to be raised again – at least not to date. Not long after this, the CCS was beset by internal wranglings which were to prove its downfall and the Society ceased to function. Restoration stopped, but essential maintenance is carried out by Derbyshire County Council. (SS)

nine

ECPDA
at Langley Mill

The Erewash Canal Preservation & Development Association was formed in 1968 to campaign against the official closure of the Erewash Canal above Tamworth Road Bridge, Long Eaton. In fact, boats continued to use the canal as far as Langley Mill, but the terminus below the road bridge was silted and unattractive. In order to provide a suitable destination for visiting boats, as well as moorings for local boat owners, ECPDA launched a successful appeal for £1,800 in 1972 to start work on excavating the Great Northern Basin of the Nottingham Canal and the lock on the Cromford Canal that gave access to it. Work began on Langley Bridge Lock 14 in 1972 with the repointing of the walls. When British Waterways bulldozed the lock cottage into the chamber in 1963 they inadvertently provided the means to reach the upper layers of brickwork without the use of ladders or scaffolding. Part of the bottom lock gates are visible above the rubble and mud, where they had been dumped and were to prove to be reusable. Beyond the lock the bed of the canal was totally infilled. (JP)

Working parties were held almost every weekend through the winter of 1972–73, removing over 4,000 tonnes of spoil, rebuilding the swing bridge across the Nottingham Canal stop lock and restoring Langley Bridge Lock. After some initial repointing had been done to the chamber walls. A Hy-Mac was used to excavate the mud and bricks and to lift out the gates. (JP)

When the heavier machinery moved in, the volunteer workforce began work at the head of the lock. At this time the limit of navigation was just the other side of the road bridge at the bottom of the lock. (JP)

The voluntary work attracted interest from many people, including no less than the then Liberal Party Leader, Jeremy Thorpe, who tried his hand at driving the mechanical excavator. (MG)

Above: By November 1972, work on Langley Bridge Lock had progressed sufficiently for the wide beam wooden clinker-built cruiser *Greta Thorden* to enter. However, the top gates and paddles were not usable at this time and the boat did not pass up the lock. The bottom gates were later rejected by British Waterways and had to be lifted out again for replanking. A small area above the lock had already been dredged out to allow boats to turn right into the Great Northern Basin at the start of the Nottingham Canal. (Harry Arnold)

Left: The official opening of the lock and the Great Northern Basin was carried out on 26 May 1973 when the Chairman of Eastwood UDC unveiled a plaque in front of a beaming Royston Torrington, Chairman of the ECPDA. (Brian Stocks)

With a brass band on one boat, several other craft in the lock and crowds all around, it was almost impossible to see the canal when the first boats for almost twenty years ceremonially passed through Langley Bridge Lock on the Cromford Canal. Amongst the boats were Mike Harrison's *Mercury,* Mick and Carole Gold's *Electra* and Royston Torrington's *Relax.* (John Wain)

The restoration did not stop with the lock, but the *modus operandi* had to change. Because British Waterways insisted that the ECPDA were not allowed to dig out any more canal unless they paid a commercial rent for it, a company had to be set up. The Langley Mill Boat Company was formed in June 1974 to dig out the infilled line of the canal and develop moorings and boatyard facilities, thus encouraging even more traffic up the underused canal. Peter Newman, Walter Maine and Michael Golds stand proudly beside the dry dock that was also built by the Langley Mill Boat Company as part of the reinstatement of the old canal. The dock measures 75ft by 23ft with a 15ft wide entrance and was first opened to boats in August 1977.

Over the years, several hundred yards have been made navigable once again, and the length in water has increased to where Beggarlee Colliery Wharf once stood. Often the original line of the canal wall was several feet below the present water level owing to mining subsidence. In this extension, the canal was dug out beyond the existing head of navigation, leaving an earth bund which is seen being removed to allow boats access to the newly available mooring area. In 2003, even more of the canal was being excavated towards the A610.

After the success of the restoration at Langley Mill, the ECPDA turned their attention to the Ironville area of the canal where silt, vegetation growth and local tipping had transformed the once attractive canal into an eyesore. During 1976 several work parties were held on the lock flight including sedge clearance below Bridge 37. (JP)

Local contractor (later Councillor) Jack Brown operates the crane-lorry he provided. The trucks were supplied by Syd West of West Transport of Ilkeston who had also provided the lorries and drivers free of charge throughout the restoration at Langley Mill. In this way far more was cleared than could have been achieved by hand. Note the old lock gates recovered from where they were dropped into the chamber by British Waterways. (JP)

Right: Dumper loads of debris, mostly deposited by less than public spirited locals, were cleared from the lock flight in December 1976 by the work parties. (MG)

Below: Lorries were filled with the accumulated rubbish of the two decades since the canal had ceased to be used. At a similar weekend work party, at the same location in February 2003, over six skipfuls of rubbish were removed at this same point by the Friends of the Cromford Canal. Formed in March 2002 to promote the restoration of the whole canal, this was their first working party and indicated a lively interest in the future of the Cromford Canal. (MG)

Friends of the Cromford Canal

In March 2002 a group of people, concerned for the future of this beautiful and historic canal, held a public meeting at Ironville. Thus was formed the Friends of the Cromford Canal (FCC) whose aim is ultimately the restoration and proper maintenance of this waterway for the benefit of all. In less than a year their membership had reached over 500, demonstrating the interest that there is – locally, nationally and internationally – in the Cromford Canal.

Readers who would like more information about the Friends of the Cromford Canal should contact Yvonne Shattower at no. 264 Bennett Street, Long Eaton, Nottingham, NG10 4JA (Tel: 0115 946 4479) or visit the web site at www.cromfordcanal.org.uk, where more images, many in colour, may be viewed, as well as further information about the canal.

Bibliography

Benjamin Outram, Reg Schofield, (Merton Priory Press, 2000, ISBN 1 898937 42 7) is a very well-researched biography of one of the Cromford Canal's main engineers and contains several chapters specifically relating to the canal.

A Walker's Guide to the Cromford Canal (FCC, 2003, ISBN 0 9544482 0 0) is just what it says in the title. It has 36 pages, is fully illustrated, and is available price £4 post paid from FCC at the above address.

Attic Appeal

Considering that boats were trading until the 1930s on both sides of Butterley Tunnel, there are remarkably few images of the Cromford Canal actually in use, and there are no known photographs of some features such as the aqueduct over the River Erewash just north of Langley Mill or that at Portland Basin. As Archivist for the Friends of the Cromford Canal, I would appeal to all readers to search their photo albums and attics for further images of the canal and to allow them to be copied for the archives and possibly for future publication. Equally if you have any memories of the canal in earlier days, I should be delighted to learn of them. If you have anything whatsoever to add to the brief story I have told, or if you find any errors in this book, please do get in touch with me:

Hugh Potter
Bankfield, Chase Road, Ambergate, Belper, DE56 2HA
(01773 852009; hugh.p@virgin.net)

C000232017

Francis Henry Durbridge

1912 and was educated at Bra~~.~~~~.~~~ ~~.~~ encouraged at an early age to write by his English teacher and went on to read English at Birmingham University. Whilst an undergraduate he started to develop the radio play format for which he first became known. At the age of twenty one he sold a play to the BBC and continued to write following his graduation whilst working as a stockbroker's clerk.

In 1938, by this time writing full time, he created the character *Paul Temple*, a crime novelist and detective. With *Steve Trent*, a Fleet Street journalist and later his wife, Temple solved numerous crimes.

Durbridge's style was very much in the mode of the earlier 'Golden Age' middle class amateur detectives . The first book, *Send for Paul Temple*, was written with John Thewes as the novelisation of a radio serial. Many others followed and they were hugely successful until the last of the series was completed in 1968. In 1969, the *Paul Temple* series was adapted for television and four of the adventures, prior to this, had been adapted for cinema, albeit with less success than radio and TV. He also invented a new character, *Tim Frazer*, an undercover agent who appeared in both novels and as a TV series.

Francis Durbridge also wrote for the stage and continued doing so up until 1991, when *Sweet Revenge* was completed. Additionally, he wrote over twenty other well received novels, most of which were on the general subject of crime. The last, Fatal Encounter, was published after his death in 1998.

Works of **Francis Durbridge** published by
HOUSE OF STRATUS

Paul Temple
&
The Harkdale
Robbery

Francis Durbridge

HOUSE OF
STRATUS

This edition published in 2011 by House of Stratus, an imprint of
Stratus Books Ltd., 21 Beeching Park, Kelly Bray,
Cornwall, PL17 8QS, UK.

www.houseofstratus.com

Typeset, printed and bound by House of Stratus.

A catalogue record for this book is available from the British Library and the Library
of Congress.

ISBN 0-7551-1906-1
EAN 978-0-7551-1906-6

CHAPTER 1

NOTHING ever happens in Harkdale on a Friday afternoon.

The black Wolseley cruised along the deserted country road because it was part of the schedule. Showing the police car in Harkdale each afternoon was like showing the flag in the outposts of empire, a symbol for the inhabitants that they were being looked after. Police Constable Newby drove through the flat midland countryside without seeing the potato fields or the pine woods; he didn't speak to P.C. Felton beside him. Newby was a town man and only the smoke and the factory skyline seven miles behind them was real. He thought of becoming a sergeant and recited pages of Moriarty's Police Law to himself to pass the time. There was nothing else to do.

"There's a lorry over there in the lay-by," said Felton.

Lay-by? He made it sound like the motorway to London. Newby reflected that it was odd for a man called Moriarty to write their basic textbook: Moriarty, the archfiend of Sherlock Holmes. For a bored few seconds he pursued the idea that the archfiend had written it all wrong to throw the law into confusion.

"Pull up, Bob," said Felton. "He might need help."

"Who might?"

"The lorry driver, of course."

Harry Felton would think of something like that! He was a born country copper, doomed to remain a P.C. all his life. He told people the time and helped old ladies across the road. The schoolkids in all these outlying villages called him Harry. He was a little undynamic for Bob Newby's taste. The police car screeched to a halt.

"So ask him if he needs help," sighed P.C. Bob Newby.

He watched his colleague go over to the lorry. 'Joseph Carter & Co.' the legend on the side of the lorry proclaimed. While somebody underneath it was tinkering with the works a fox terrier guarded the dismantled rear wheel. The hub and various parts of the wheel were scattered over the grass verge.

"Hello, Jackson," said the policeman as he bent down to pat the dog. The dog, Jackson, wagged its tail. "Are you having trouble?" Even the damned dogs, Bob Newby realised, knew Harry Felton. "Where's your villain of a master?"

The dog's master looked a villain to P.C. Newby, but then most people did to P.C. Newby. The lorry driver didn't look, apart from the way he was dressed, like a lorry driver. He looked an intelligent young man, but he had longish hair; his attitude as he stood up beside the lorry was slightly supercilious. He looked like the kind of student who gets arrested on demonstrations.

"Hello, Gavin," P.C. Felton said. "Fancy seeing you."

"Enjoying a spot of lunch," said the young man with a glance at his watch. Then he spoke to the dog: "We enjoyed our scampi and avocado pear, didn't we, Jackson?"

The dog leaped up at its master as P.C. Newby strolled across to join them. "You look as if you're in trouble, mate," Newby said, making it sound slightly ambiguous. But Gavin Renson accepted the edge of menace cheerfully.

"I'm always in trouble, aren't I, Harry?"

Felton nodded amiably. "How long have you been working for Carter's?"

"Just over a week."

"Ah, temporary, is it?"

"Yes," Gavin Renson agreed with a laugh, "bloody temporary.

Look at the lorry they gave me."

Newby sniffed irritably. As a policeman he knew what he liked, and he didn't like Gavin Renson. "Is there anything we can do for you?" he asked.

"Well, that's kind of you. Yes, I think I need a new job. But a nice soft cushy job this time."

"A job like mine, I take it?" Newby snapped.

"Well, you said it!"

Gavin Renson clearly preferred policemen who gave him the feed lines. He looked disappointed when Harry Felton intervened with a diplomatic, "I doubt whether we've a uniform that would fit your lanky figure. And Jackson isn't a standard sized police dog. Too short, and he has small feet."

Newby watched angrily while Gavin Renson conferred with his dog about mixing with all those undesirable Alsatians.

"Do Carter's know about this breakdown?" he asked sharply.

"Yes, I've been on the blower. They're sending someone—"

"Okay, so there's nothing we can do." Newby turned away. "Come on, Harry," he called.

They drove away through the flat countryside. A Cortina passed them going in the opposite direction and Newby wondered incredulously what business a man could have in Harkdale. The tiny town had gradually appeared on the horizon while Harry Felton was talking. It was a farm town and once a week, on Fridays, it came to something like life, when the farmers brought in their wares to market. Even that was a dying tradition, Newby thought, thank God.

"It was only boy's stuff. Stealing lead off a church roof, I think, nothing serious. He got caught because he took the dog with him. But these things stick in a small town, so he never lasts long in a regular job. He's known as a wide boy. The last job he had was with Kimber's in Banbury."

"The estate agents?" Newby asked absently.

"That's right. He was there nearly six months. I gather he did quite well at the beginning, but eventually they had to get rid of him." Harry Felton laughed. "It was the usual story. He would insist on having the dog with him all the time!"

Newby grinned. "Why does he call it Jackson?"

"I don't know." Felton shrugged. "It's always been called Jackson."

They had reached Harkdale and were driving through the main street. There was a Woolworths, a new supermarket, and a number of bay windowed shops selling afternoon tea, women's clothes, and an old established firm of solicitors. Outside the bank there was a Ford Zephyr and a small knot of people were watching three men coming out of the building. Just as deserted as always, Newby thought, six people and two cars in the whole High Street. The three men coming out of the bank were carrying guns and their faces were covered by nylon stockings.

"Good God, Harry! Look at that!"

The tallest man was wearing a suede jacket and grey flannel trousers. He was carrying a large leather bag.

"What's going on?" Harry asked in amazement as the bell started ringing inside the bank.

The bell was a signal for the slow motion scene to erupt. The small knot of people watching suddenly scattered. It was real, and they were in danger. A frantic clerk came running, shouting and waving his arms, from the bank. The tall man tossed the bag into.the car, then turned and shot the clerk.

"Let's move," grunted Newby.

Harry Felton accelerated across the street and swung the police car across to block their escape. He came to a halt with his front wheels on the pavement. Newby could hear two women screaming as he reached for his radio telephone, and a man was shouting, "Don't be a fool!" Felton leaped out of the car.

The three bank robbers were in the Zephyr and it was backing wildly to turn and make its escape. Harry Felton ran into the road but it drove straight at him. He threw himself clear at the last moment. By the time he had regained his feet the Zephyr had finished its three-point turn.

The next two seconds passed very slowly for P.C. Newby. He watched Harry Felton put out a hand to seize the passenger door, and the tall bank robber leaned out of the window, carefully pointed his gun at Harry's stomach, and fired three times. Harry Felton toppled balletically onto the road, twitched twice and then lay still. As Newby knelt beside him the Zephyr sped off through the deserted High Street.

Newby wished the bloody alarm bell would stop ringing. But it brought out a few more people as soon as the street was safe. A doctor appeared and pushed his way through the sightseers to attend the bank clerk. Harry Felton was dead. Newby went across to the doctor.

"Have you radioed for an ambulance?" the doctor asked.

"That's what I was doing while my mate was getting killed."

The doctor nodded. "This one will live."

The bank clerk was conscious and babbling with the pain from his shoulder. The blood from his clawing hands mingled with tears so that his face became streaked with red and dirt. The manager of the bank had emerged at last to demand that somebody should do something.

"Get after them," he blustered at Newby. "They've stolen nearly fifty thousand pounds!"

Newby glared. "Don't worry, we'll get them." He turned and went back to Harry Felton's body, before he could say anything he might regret. He could hear the siren of a police car in the distance, a black Jaguar doing what seemed to be ninety miles an hour. Within seconds it had skidded to a stop beside Newby.

Police Constable Brooks slid from the driving seat as it

stopped. "How much start have they had?" he asked.

"A minute or so," murmured Newby.

P.C. Brooks looked down at the dead policeman. "We'll catch up with them." He put a hand on Newby's shoulder. "Harry was a good lad."

"Harry Felton was a fool and he got on my nerves but he was the nicest guy in the world."

"Leave it to me," said Brooks.

He slipped back into the car, slammed the door and turned the ignition key all in the same movement, leaving P.C. Newby standing forlorn by the dead man. His speedometer was flickering around ninety again within fifteen seconds. He was a fast driver, and Bill Stanton sat next to him with his eyes closed. When they reached the open road and accelerated to a hundred and twenty miles an hour Stanton's lips began moving in prayer.

"Harry Felton was a nice bloke," Brooks said bitterly. "He never harmed anyone."

"Concentrate on the road," Stanton muttered.

"I'm going as fast as I can."

"I know."

Constable Horace Brooks was a dark, determined man in his late thirties. He had steel nerves and his list of commendations for bravery was almost as long as the list of cars he had crashed in the line of duty. Promotion had escaped him because he conducted his own one-man crusade against crime and police discipline. Only his charm and an engaging record of success had kept him in the force.

"There she is," he said grimly. "About three miles in front."

Far away in the grey distance a Ford Zephyr was going too fast and throwing up a cloud of dust.

"We'll be there before they hit town."

Brooks glanced out of the corner of his eye at a lorry parked in the lay-by. A man and a dog were standing watching them go by, and then in his driving mirror Brooks saw the man climb with the dog into his driving cabin.

"Look where you're going," said Stanton. "The road starts winding soon."

"I can see."

They were gaining rapidly on the Zephyr but Brooks didn't dare let up; once the Zephyr reached town it would be a much simpler matter to double back through the busy streets and lose them. The two cars raced along the gradually winding road, tyres screaming and back wheels slithering into the verge.

"Thank God for the winding road," Brooks called. "They won't be able to use their guns on us now."

"God help us," muttered Stanton.

There was a farm on their right, and several seconds before the crash Brooks saw what was going to happen. A tractor was coming out of the fields; almost immediately he lost sight of it behind the farmhouse, and then as they sped past the farmhouse and round the corner Brooks saw the tractor lurch into the road. The Ford Zephyr skidded nearly twenty yards before hitting the tractor with a bang that sounded like an atomic explosion. The tractor disintegrated and came to rest in a muddle of twisted metal in the opposite ditch. The Ford Zephyr spun on until it hit a tree.

"God help us."

Brooks had slowed down. He manoeuvred the car perilously past the moving wreckage and managed to stop a hundred yards further on. Stanton threw open his passenger door and stumbled into the road.

"Fat lot we can do to help them," Brooks said grimly. He picked up the radio telephone to report in. Then he noticed that Stanton was being sick on the grass verge. At that moment the tractor's petrol tank burst into flames.

P.C. Horace Brooks walked slowly back to the remains of the

Zephyr. He had no real desire to examine the crumpled, broken bodies trapped inside the wreckage. One man was screaming hysterically, screaming that his legs were gone, screaming for quick death. The others seemed to be dead already.

Brooks spent several minutes hunting for the driver of the tractor, and eventually he found the man's body in the field beyond the ditch. He was still alive, miraculously. To judge from the blood he had crawled about two yards and then lost consciousness.

"You'll never believe it," Horace Brooks said to a sickly looking P.C. Stanton, "but this is why I hate driving too fast. There are too many people about who should never be allowed behind a wheel."

Stanton was making soothing noises to the man who had lost his legs, trying to calm him until the ambulance arrived. Horace Brooks shrugged gloomily, lit a cigarette, and sat on the grass to wait.

Half an hour later the scene was crowded. Two ambulances, a breakdown lorry and another police car had arrived to clear the debris. A police photographer and a young reporter from the local press had asked questions of everybody in sight, and a dozen people had materialised on the deserted road to provide an audience. P.C. Brooks was reporting to his inspector.

"The tall man's name is Thorne," he explained, "Oscar Thorne. They call him Skibby for some reason." He led the thick set, morose inspector from the ambulance back to the wrecked car. A man was using an oxyacetylene cutter to free one of the corpses. "But all these men are just thugs," he said, "they're hoodlums. They wouldn't know how to plan a bank raid."

Detective Inspector Manley nodded. He was too busy trying to light his pipe to answer the constable. At last he waved away a cloud of smoke and coughed. "They may not have planned it, but they're ruthlessly efficient. This is the third bank robbery in this part of the county in two weeks."

"Well, they didn't get away with the money this time."

P.C. Stanton had retrieved the large black leather bag from the Zephyr. "Do you want to take charge of this, sir?" he asked the inspector.

"Yes, I'll take it back to the station." Inspector Manley took the bag and returned to his own car. He put the bag on the passenger seat and climbed in behind the wheel. "Report back to me as soon as this mess has been cleared up," he called to P.C. Brooks.

"Aye aye, sir."

Inspector Manley switched on the ignition and put the car into gear. Then he changed his mind and switched off. Curiosity had got the better of him. He took the black leather bag and applied a small penknife to the lock. It sprang open.

Manley stared in bewilderment at a copy of the Concise Oxford Dictionary. That was all the bag contained. The money was gone.

"Another of the men whom the police wished to question in relation to the bank robbery yesterday afternoon at Harkdale has died, it was reported early this morning. The man was forty-three-year-old Oscar Thorne, described as a garage proprietor from south London. This brings the total number of deaths arising out of the robbery to four, and police sources say that the fifty thousand pound haul has still not been recovered—"

Desmond Blane switched off the radio as he climbed down the steps of the caravan into the field. He could still hear the newsreader's voice droning in the next caravan. "The young widow of P.C. Harry Felton said last night—" The heart strings in twenty-four caravans all the way to the edge of the 'farm' were probably being pulled by the young girl's tragic bereavement. Desmond Blane sat on the bottom step and stared aggressively at the frost coloured grass.

Bloody farm indeed, he thought, it's just a stretch of marsh land where nothing would grow and cows would sink into the ground if they stayed still. The Red Trees Caravan Site! He wondered whether to get dressed. It was cold to be hanging around in pyjamas and a silk dressing gown, and the matching silk scarf wasn't keeping death from laryngitis at bay.

He looked up as he heard somebody whistling. It was Arnold Cookson, threading his way cheerfully through the neighbouring caravans with two pints of milk in his hands.

"Where the hell have you been?" Desmond Blane asked roughly.

"Up to the farmhouse."

"I've just heard the radio. Skibby's dead."

"Oh." Arnold Cookson pursed his lips in a silent whistle. He was a much older man, in his early sixties perhaps, and he seemed upset by the news. "What about Larry and Ray?" he asked.

"They weren't mentioned."

Arnold Cookson pushed past him into the caravan. He poured some milk into a saucepan and lit the Calor gas ring. He was preparing breakfast.

"Why does a farm sell milk in milk bottles?"

"I don't know." Arnold examined the milk bottle. "Perhaps it's a good thing," he said, almost to himself. "Skibby would have talked."

"So what makes you think Ray will keep his big mouth shut?" Blane spoke loudly, blustering with nerves. "Once they start asking him awkward questions—" His voice faded into silence. "Who's this?"

There was a lorry bumping its way noisily down the lane to the caravan site. 'Joseph Carter & Co.' it proclaimed on the side. Blane walked suspiciously across to the gate.

"We weren't expecting you until this afternoon," he called.

Gavin Renson jumped cheerfully from the driving cabin. "I know, but we thought we'd come for breakfast." He took a large black leather bag from the tool compartment under his seat and strolled past Blane towards the caravan.

"Come on, Jackson," he called to the dog. "Come and have your porridge."

CHAPTER 2

PAUL TEMPLE tried to relax in the tip-up chair; he closed his eyes while the girl clattered her implements about on the ledge by his head. She adjusted the chair slightly and shone the light full in his face. It was like being at the dentists, except that Miss Benson was younger and prettier than any dentist Paul had been treated by. And she made him feel much more nervous. He didn't feel happy having his face made up.

"Do I have to be made up like this?" Paul protested as a matter of form.

"Oh yes, it's terribly hot under the lights. You'll perspire, and we wouldn't want you to look shiny, would we?"

"Heaven forbid."

Miss Benson put the finishing touches to his lips, patted his face with powder and then whipped away the towel from under his chin. "There, now you look like an extremely well preserved novelist."

He rose from the chair and scowled. "I am an extremely well preserved novelist."

"Exactly."

Another girl popped her head round the door, exactly on cue, and said, "Are you ready for Hospitality now, Mr. Temple?"

"I suppose so."

Paul waved a resigned farewell to Miss Benson and followed the second girl to a room at the end of the corridor. Four brightly attractive young ladies were chatting up four nervous

12

middle aged men.

"My name's Andrea Turberville," Paul's bright young lady told him. "I gather you've been through all this before."

"Yes. What happens next is that you conjure up a very large whisky and ginger wine."

"That's right," she said, "and a small sherry for me." In fact they were conjured up by a chirpy young man. "Not nervous, are you?" Andrea asked.

"Terrified." He wasn't, but it seemed the right thing to say. Paul didn't want to appear blasé. "I'm always tempted on occasions like these to hire a professional actor, so that he can project his personality and remember all the witty lines I think of afterwards. Do you know any good professional actors?"

She laughed as if it were all part of her job.

"Don't worry. Brian's terribly good at putting people at their ease. He'll help you out if you forget the title of your latest novel or if you suddenly become convinced that your flies are undone. Brian's terribly professional."

Paul glanced cautiously down at his trousers.

"By the way, have you met your fellow performers? Let me introduce you—"

Brian Clay conducted a chat programme for ITV that aspired to treat serious subjects in a serious way between interludes of pop song and dance. The serious subject this week was crime. Paul Temple had just written a series of newspaper articles in which he claimed that crime was no longer a haphazard collection of underdogs dabbling in a spot of burglary, as it had been, but an organised business with no place for the amateur. So Paul Temple was on the show.

He would be talking to Freddy the Drummer, a man who had spent most of his life in and out of approved schools, borstals and gaol, to a retired agent of M.I.5 or M.I.6, nobody seemed sure which, and to an elderly M.P. who wanted to bring back the birch and arm the police.

Paul said hello to them and mentioned the weather. It would take all of Brian Clay's well known sincerity and charm to produce brilliant talk from this bunch of egotists, Paul decided. The M.P. was talking as if he feared that once he paused for breath somebody else might speak, and the braying tones were designed to wake up apathetic voters at the back of the hall.

"What do you think of this circus?" Paul asked the M.I.5 or 6 agent.

"I think everybody's terribly talented and sincere," he said absently. His brightly attractive young lady was keeping him primed with a continuous supply of whisky. "Terribly professional."

Paul nodded and wondered whether to talk instead to Freddie the Drummer. But Freddie was sprawled in an armchair, sprawling lower and lower in an attempt to get a better view of Andrea's mini skirt.

"I think it's time we went onto the set," said Andrea Turberville. "It's a few minutes early, but we ought to see you under the lights. I'll take you to Richard Cross. He's the director."

The set was the usual table surrounded by armchairs. There was water in carafes and there were ashtrays everyone was told not to use while on camera. Andrea sat them all down to face a tiered audience of two hundred people. There was a stage over to the right where the dancers would dance, and behind the stage a dance band was playing to warm up the audience.

"Paul Temple, eh?" barked the M.P. He had sat in the next armchair. "I suppose you writer chaps have been hit by the abolition of capital punishment. No dragging off the villain at the end of the piece. Who cares who dun it when the fellow just goes and spends the rest of his life in comfort at the expense of the ratepayer?"

Richard Cross scurried across the studio to welcome them all. He said that it should be a terribly controversial programme and Brian was thrilled to have them all on the show. "I think we'll start with Paul's thesis about big business, is that all right, Paul? And then we'll talk about how the police aren't really equipped to cope with such streamlined organisation, and we'll talk about spies and undercover work. It'll be riveting. The milk will boil over in a million homes. Any questions?"

"Yes," said the man from Intelligence. "What happened to that little dolly with the whisky?"

Richard Cross gave a faintly distraught laugh.

The Melody Girls had been rehearsing on the stage to the right, and Paul noticed that one of them had remained on the set. She was a tall redhead with strikingly troubled green eyes. Paul thought that she was coming across to them, but somebody called her, and after a moment's hesitation she went away. Her green flaired chiffon costume was too brief to be hanging around in draughts.

"Sir Michael," the director said to the M.P., "I wonder whether you'd change places with Paul? Your spectacles are upsetting camera number two. Miss Benson! Where's Miss Benson? Freddie the Drummer needs some powder on his bald patch—"

The audience suddenly applauded as a dark, moodily intense young man walked onto the set. He was dressed in a dramatic black suit with white frills, and the one touch of colour was his floppy red bow tie. Without looking across he waved a languid hand in acknowledgment of the clapping. "Hi," he said to his guests in general. "Great to see you, marvellous. It'll be a great programme." He was Brian Clay.

"We're on in ninety seconds, Brian," said the director.

"Great." The super-cool young man sat in the centre seat behind the desk and smiled dramatically. "Hi," he said to Freddie the Drummer, "great to have you out in time for the programme. Paul! How nice to have you on the show." He leaned across and offered a languid hand. "I thought your last

15

book was great."

Paul beamed complacently. The nice thing about being flattered by Brian Clay was that he bothered to do it. Clay had the art of seeming to bestow a royal favour, which was warming for the brief moment it lasted. He was terribly sincere. But while Paul was grinning at the military intelligence agent in private amusement they had gone on the air.

"Hi," Brian Clay was saying, "and good evening. Tonight we're going to discuss one of the central, most real threats to our health and security, one of the most dramatic aspects of the world today. I'm talking about crime, and the way it is likely to touch us all in the next ten years, because it's the fastest growing disease in our society. It no longer only happens to other people—"

His voice was faintly rasping, as if the menace were there among them. "And here to discuss it with us tonight—" He was a professional. He had all the sensational statistics on cards before him, and his intensity would have quite a few old ladies glancing over their shoulders at the back door. "Mr. Paul Temple, crime writer and in his own way, criminologist!"

A man over to the right waved and the audience applauded. Paul glanced down in sudden apprehension at his trousers.

"Paul, tell me what's so different about this present situation. Is it simply that crime is better organised, or is it different? Change or development?" He stared so innocently that Paul felt a serious answer was required. "Mm?"

"What is different is that the people who get caught these days are not the real criminals. In the past if you caught a gang of bank robbers and sent them to gaol that was it, those criminals were out of harm's way for several years. But these days – these days the gang gets caught if you're lucky, but the brain behind the crime is left free to plan his next big job. The men behind organised crime are never caught. So no matter how many petty villains you send to gaol you don't improve the situation. You only fill up the gaols with petty villains."

"That's a disturbing thought, Paul." He turned dramatically to the M.P. "Sir Michael, I know you think our present laws make it all too easy for the criminals."

The M.P. began with heavy facetiousness about his role as a Clay pigeon, and then he laughed lugubriously. On the stage to their right The Melody Girls were assembling for their routine. Paul found his attention straying. He didn't think that the fervour with which M.P.s held their opinions indicated their profundity. Sir Michael was a bore. Yet the red-headed girl was watching them without a thought for the coming dance number.

"Paul, what do you think about that?"

"Eh?" The wretch had sprung it on him deliberately. "I think Sir Michael is very sincere," Paul said, "but he knows very little about criminals." He wished he had heard a word Sir Michael had said. "A prominent M.P.'s life may be very worthy, but it doesn't equip a man to understand what makes a criminal tick. There's a fantastic difference between the lives of the law givers and the law receivers, and I think Sir Michael personifies that difference."

Brian Clay perked up at the prospect of some real television, while Sir Michael spluttered with astonishment.

"I keep in touch with the people," he shouted, "through my constituents! I know my people and what they think! This weekend I'll be back there holding my monthly clinic, and what will you be doing, writing a novel?"

Paul nodded happily. "I'm going off to the cottage, actually, and I hope to start on my new book—"

"Cottage? You retreat to a cottage in the country and talk to me about crime? What happens in your part of the country? They probably don't know what crime is!"

"Freddie, where do you sit on this fence?" Brian Clay asked.

"Yes, well, I mean, they're right, aren't they? What happens in country cottages? And how would an M.P. know about crime?"

"Does that worry you?" Brian Clay asked the man from Intelligence. "Did you used to feel there was a gulf between the life of the pursuer and the pursued?"

"Never." The impeccably dressed man smiled beatifically. "What I always say is that if you're still alive then you haven't much to worry about, have you?"

That was a conversation stopper. While Brian Clay worked out how to begin again the director waved to the dancers. They were all in place and the music began its introduction.

"Ladies and gentlemen," Brian murmured into the microphone, "we give you The Melody Girls!"

The show went out live at ten o'clock on a Friday evening. Doing it live ensured spontaneity and the extra charge of tension which Brian Clay thought so essential to real television. It also meant it was damned late when Paul left the studios. The clock in the gatekeeper's lodge showed two minutes past eleven. Paul waved in farewell to the man from Intelligence, who tottered off in search of a drink, and looked about for his car.

"Paul! Over here!"

His wife waved while the gatekeeper raised the barrier. She was looking brightly enthusiastic, so presumably she had approved of his performance. Paul slipped into the passenger seat and kissed her on the cheek.

"Was I all right?" he asked.

"Marvellous, darling. You were terribly sincere."

"Oh my God."

Steve had insisted on watching the programme in the saloon bar of the pub round the corner from the studio. It was her idea of a public opinion sample. And the pub had a colour set.

"The people in the saloon bar enjoyed the way you made Sir Michael look ridiculous. But of course they all agreed with him."

Paul sighed. "Well, let's get moving. We've a long way to go tonight."

Steve pressed the accelerator and they moved out into the traffic. By the main entrance to the studios Paul saw the red headed dancer struggling with her suitcase. As they drove past the girl swung round to look at them, tripped over the case and fell.

"Pull up!" Paul exclaimed.

"I thought," Steve said with an ironic glance at the girl, "we had a long way to go."

"Something's bothering that girl."

"I remember the feeling when I first met you."

Paul hurried back along the pavement and helped the girl to her feet. She was more embarrassed than hurt. Paul picked up the suitcase and watched while she brushed the dust off her coat.

"Are you all right now?"

"No, I've laddered my stockings."

"Perhaps we can give you a lift somewhere?"

She smiled gratefully. "I was hoping to catch the eleven thirty from Paddington. It's the last train—"

"We'll make it." Paul put the suitcase in the boot of the Rolls and then held the door while she climbed into the back of the car. "Where are you going?"

"Oxford," she said. "My parents live near there and I promised to spend the night with them. For a change. I haven't seen them in months."

"This is your lucky night," murmured Steve. She drove into the main flow of traffic going out to the Western Avenue. "We're off to the Cotswolds, so we can drop you off at your door. We've a house near Broadway."

"It's awfully kind of you." The girl relaxed, removed her hat and tossed the red hair free, then she smiled. "I'm Betty

Stanway, by the way. I'm a dancer."

"Steve Temple. And the man with the charming manners is my husband."

"I know, I was in the Brian Clay Show with him. I was meaning to talk to him all evening, but my nerve kept failing me. I know it must be tiresome for celebrities to have complete strangers button-holing them; I don't usually do it."

"What did you want to talk to him about?" Steve asked. "Paul enjoys being button-holed by attractive young dancers."

"I wanted to ask his advice. Or at least, well, I wanted to give him some information. You know, I just felt I needed to talk to someone, and after I read that series of articles in the newspaper—" She had become incoherent. "I was worried, that's all."

"Have you eaten today, Miss Stanway?" Steve asked, briskly maternal and down to earth.

The girl was startled. "No, I don't think so."

"Neither has Paul. He pretends to be absolutely blasé about his television appearances, but he's so nervous he doesn't eat for two days beforehand. We'll stop at the Coach Club. We can have supper, and they serve drinks there until three in the morning. All right, Paul?"

"Good idea." Paul watched the lights of the oncoming traffic. "But I wasn't nervous. I had two hamburgers at half past seven this evening."

The Coach House was an eighteenth century building on the outskirts of Oxford. It had its legends as a meeting place for the literary establishment from Byron to Beerbohm, but it was now the haunt of motor car executives and the more pampered undergraduates. Paul led the two women into the dining room. It was only half full, but the aroma of rich food and cigars hung in the air. The oak beams and brass looked decently timeless in the half light. It could have been any time since 1732, apart from the clothes.

"Good evening, Mr. Temple. Will your party stay at the bar while we take your order?"

"Thank you, Bilson, I think we will." He turned to Betty Stanway. "What would you like, Miss Stanway?"

"Oh, Betty, please," she gasped. "A dry martini, please. Everyone calls me Betty."

"Three dry martinis, please, Bilson."

"Yes, sir."

They sat in comfortable leather armchairs. Paul hoped he wouldn't become too comfortable and fall asleep. It had been a full day, and the mood of the Coach House was calculatedly euphoric.

"Talk to me, Betty," he said. "Tell me all your worries."

As Betty took her drink from the bartender the slightly red light turned her eyes into a dramatic violet colour. "I read all those articles you wrote about the recent bank robberies and the way crime has changed. Like you were saying tonight. You said that the people who actually committed the robberies were not the people—"

Paul nodded his encouragement. "Not necessarily the people who organised them. That was what I said in the paper, and after this Harkdale affair I'm more than ever convinced that I'm right. Because most of the people who committed that robbery are dead, and the money is still missing."

"I know." She put her glass down in a sudden, unladylike gesture. "I know something about what happened at Harkdale. Not much. It isn't enough to go to the police with, and I'm not the kind who goes to the police in any case. But I think I heard the robbery being planned."

"Go on, Betty." He wasn't tired any more. "Start at the beginning."

"Well, for the last six months I've been working at a club called The Love-Inn. That's where The Melody Girls were formed. I don't suppose you would know it—"

"It's in Soho; owned by a woman called Rita Fletcher."

"That's right. You are well informed. Although actually it's run by Rita for the man who really owns it. He's an American, a horrible little dipso. Rita runs it for him. But anyway, one night, about three months ago, Rita introduced me to a man called Desmond Blane—"

CHAPTER 3

ONE night about three months ago Rita Fletcher had introduced her to a man called Desmond Blane. He was a wealthy man, or he lived like one, which amounted to the same thing. Betty had already noticed him in the club several times and she encouraged his friendship. Betty Stanway wasn't hoping to be a dancer all her life.

Desmond Blane was in his early thirties, a powerfully built dark haired man. He lived in Knightsbridge, which seemed to Betty the height of aristocratic living. He called it a penthouse and it overlooked the park. Betty was too impressed to ask what he did for a living. She assumed it was something in the City.

The third time she spent the night at his penthouse she developed doubts about the City. They had gone to bed rather late even for her, she was exhausted and high on vodka. She scarcely remembered going to bed, and when she woke up it was daylight and Desmond was not beside her.

She lay there for a few minutes trying to piece together what had happened the night before. She was afraid she might have fallen asleep while they were making love. Betty wasn't terribly good at the fast life. She needed a cup of coffee.

When Desmond appeared in his silk dressing gown and matching silk scarf, looking like a bachelor from a more serious 1920's musical, he was reading the morning's mail.

"Good morning," she murmured with an anxious smile.

"Oh, you're awake." He confirmed her worst imaginings;

instead of reassuring her Desmond ripped open a letter with obvious displeasure.

"I'd love some coffee."

"I made some," he said absent mindedly. "It's in the kitchen."

When Betty returned with a cup of coffee Desmond was still sitting on the foot of the bed with the letter in his hand.

"What's the matter, Des?" she asked. "Bad news?"

"No, it's nothing." He put the letter in his dressing gown pocket. "Just business. Isn't it time you put some clothes on?"

"I'm sorry, Des." Something told her it was all spoiled. Last night they had talked of going away for the weekend. It was her first long weekend free in ages, and they were going to spend it together. But that had been last night. Betty picked up her clothes and went into the dressing room. Now it was morning.

She was twenty-eight, and she was beginning to dread the mornings. She was too often hung over, and every morning the crow's feet looked more noticeable around her eyes. She touched her toes twelve times, splashed cold water on her breasts and breathed deeply by the open window. It would be nice to be young again, or middle aged and past all this. It would be nice to be a shorthand typist.

She was massaging her neck with cream when she realised that Desmond was talking in the bedroom. Her natural curiosity triumphed over discretion.

"I'm not happy about it," he was saying. "You know damned well why. In my opinion we're pushing fate."

Betty crouched and peered through the keyhole but she could only see his feet tapping in agitation on the floor. His large blue slippers looked absurdly like separate beings, dancing together, nothing to do with the man.

"Have you spoken to Renson? And what about Skibby? What does he think?" There was a pause. "He would, the greedy bastard. But I still think the twenty-third is too soon after the other jobs. And why Harkdale? I don't even know where Harkdale is!"

Betty went through into the bedroom. Desmond Blane didn't even look up at her.

"All right, we'll talk about it tonight. Yes, yes, we'll discuss it. I'll see you about eight o'clock."

Betty went across to him and put her arms round his neck from behind. "Who was that," she asked with a laboured attempt at humour, "another one of your girlfriends?"

"Mm?" He suddenly smiled at her. He was back. "Yes, an impatient Spanish bird. I call her my flaming flamingo." He kissed her neck. "But she can't dance the way you dance, Elizabeth, and she lacks your stamina."

Betty laughed delightedly. "Do you really love me, Des? You said last night—Well, you said we could go away together for the weekend.

"We'll have the wildest weekend of your life," he said deliberately. "Be here on Friday morning at ten o'clock sharp, and bring your passport. It will be a weekend to remember."

Friday mornings in Knightsbridge are pretty crowded and the taxi pulled up outside the block of service flats at four minutes past ten. Betty emerged from the taxi in her smart little powder lemon suit and carrying her weekend case. She paid off the taxi and hurried into the entrance. Desmond Blane's flat was on the fifth floor and she waited for the lift.

"Good morning, miss," said the porter. "Going up?"

"Fifth floor, please. It's a beautiful morning. It's going to be a beautiful weekend."

"Yes, miss." The old boy slammed the gates and they shot up in a vertical take-off. He clearly enjoyed his work. "If you're wanting Mr. Blane I don't think he's in."

"Oh yes," said Betty, "he's expecting me." She had received a note from Desmond the day before, urging her to be on time and reminding her to bring her passport.

"Fifth floor," he announced defiantly. "But Mr. Blane isn't in."

Betty went along the corridor to the front door of Desmond's flat and rang the bell. She rang again almost immediately. The elderly porter had remained with the lift and he was watching with satisfaction. She banged on the door with her fist.

"He hasn't been here since Monday night!" the porter bawled.

Betty walked slowly back to the lift.

"And he's not coming back neither," the old boy added, "not never."

"Are you sure?" She went into the lift; the clang of the gates and then the plunge to the ground seemed absurdly symbolic to her. "There must be some mistake."

"No, miss. The head porter, he had a note from the agents this morning. We got the keys back, and there's talk of another tenant moving in on Monday. There isn't no mistake."

"But his clothes—the furniture—I mean, did he move out?"

The old man shrugged. "These flats are all let furnished. I suppose he just took his clothes and personal belongings." He watched her leave the lift and walk unhappily back to the street and his satisfaction waned. "I'm sorry, miss," he said finally. "It came as a bit of a surprise to us as well. He'd been here three years. It was a bit sudden."

"Never mind," she murmured. "I've been stood up before." She tried to smile. "I suppose you're working this weekend?"

"Yes, I'm afraid so." He grinned. "But you'll have a beautiful weekend."

During the next three weeks Betty Stanway forgot Desmond Blane. She was a resilient girl and men still noticed her. The shoulder length auburn hair and the lithe dancer's body attracted enough admiration to make the evenings fun. And then all the girls were going to appear on television, which meant extra rehearsals and a lot of hard work. They had been on television several times in the past five years, but Betty still experienced a naive feeling of excitement: maybe this would be her breakthrough, the girls featured on a regular show each week, eventual main billing, stardom. At one o'clock in the morning the fantasy would take hold, and it did no harm. She even began to feel fit, almost human, when she woke up. Until the morning when she saw a report in the newspaper about a robbery in Harkdale.

Then she remembered the telephone call which Desmond had been making that morning before he disappeared. He hadn't even known where Harkdale was! Betty glanced at the date on the newspaper. It was the twenty-fourth, and the robbery had been on the twenty-third. She read through the report again. It just couldn't be coincidence.

While she was dressing she turned on the radio. The rehearsal had been called for ten o'clock so she had no time to worry about ex-boyfriends. She put Harkdale out of her mind until the news came on.

"Another of the men whom the police wished to question in relation to the bank robbery yesterday afternoon at Harkdale has died, it was reported early this morning. The man was forty-three-year-old Oscar Thorne—"

Betty went to work in a trance. She caught the tube at Belsize Park as usual, accepted a seat with a smile from an elderly business man, and sat staring at the black pipes in the tunnel. She wondered whether to go to the police, but she had nothing to tell them except a name, and that might seem like malice against the man who had jilted her. She lit a cigarette and read unseeingly through the rest of the newspaper. Protest demonstrations, war in Asia, a couple of sexual assaults, politicians denouncing racialism. Nothing to capture the attention. Her mind wandered on to an article about the new brains behind organised crime.

"What Rothschild did to banking and Woolworth did to shopkeeping Al Capone did to crime, but Al Capone was not a brilliant man. Today the rewards of crime are comparable to those of other big business careers, and a brilliant tycoon might waver before deciding to become a property developer. And at least three tycoons have decided otherwise—"

Betty read with total absorption and almost forgot to change trains at Tottenham Court Road. She knew that Desmond wasn't a tycoon of crime, because he had been protesting against the instructions he had received from someone. But she was pleased to have it confirmed that he was a business man. The article went on to question the effectiveness of a police force drawn from a basically underprivileged section of society, who could no more cope with modern crime than they could cope with irregularities in high finance.

The author was Paul Temple. In the last few lines of his article he mentioned the Harkdale robbery as proof of his argument. The series of articles had obviously been written well in advance, and the reference to Harkdale would have been a last minute insertion. Betty was impressed, especially when she arrived at the television studios and found that Paul Temple was to be a star guest in the Brian Clay Show that evening. She determined to tell him what had happened.

It would be easier to talk to a stranger than to someone she knew, even someone as close as Rita Fletcher. Rita came to the rehearsal for about an hour in the afternoon, and she sensed that something was wrong. But Betty couldn't talk to her.

"I'm depressed, I suppose," said Betty. "There's nothing wrong."

"You girls are always down about something. Are these men worth it? I wish they didn't exist!" Rita was an extrovert woman in her mid-forties, and clearly men never gave her any trouble. She was bosomy and corsetted and her men did as she told them. "You need a rest. You ought to go home to mother for the weekend. On Monday you'll be a new girl."

"It's all right, Rita—"

"Go home. Mr. Coley won't miss you for two days."

Betty nodded gratefully. She hadn't been home since Christmas. Maybe she could leave her problems behind in London. "I'll telephone my mother during the break."

She almost went home without talking to Paul Temple. He was a debonair type, smoothly relaxed with all the terrifying television people. As the evening wore on Betty's resolution began to fail. She tried to speak to him twice, but he was always surrounded by producers and people like that. He had an amused manner which helped to make some politician Betty had never heard of look ridiculous. Even though Paul Temple smiled at her rather sweetly the things she had to say about Harkdale seemed too trivial, and she didn't want to look a fool.

Then as she was leaving the studios she had seen him being driven away by a woman who didn't look much older than herself. Betty had swung round in indecision and fallen across her suitcase. That was how she came to tell Paul Temple her troubles. [They gave her a lift to Oxford. She told her story over a succulent steak at the Coach House.]

"Desmond seems to have completely disappeared," she concluded. "When I read about the robbery in Harkdale, and the man who was killed, the man they called Skibby, I realised what had happened."

Paul Temple nodded in encouragement. "Tell me, Betty, did you ever meet any of Blane's friends? Renson, or the man called Skibby, for instance?"

"No," she said, "I'd never heard of them before that phone call."

His wife, Steve, looked disappointed. "But surely you must have met some of his friends?"

29

"I know it's peculiar now that you mention it, but I didn't. We went out quite a lot, but always it was only the two of us." She finished the steak, and felt contentedly full. The club itself impressed her. "Actually Rita came with us on one occasion. It was a Sunday and the three of us drove out to Maidenhead for lunch."

"When Desmond came to the club, to the Love-Inn, was he always alone?" Steve asked.

"Yes, always. Except on New Year's Eve." Betty suddenly remembered the occasion, it was almost the first time she had met Desmond Blane. Most of the members had been drunk and Cynthia Elphinstone had nearly been sacked for doing a strip tease to Auld Lang Syne. "He had another man with him that night, a man called Arnold something or other. I didn't like him very much. He stared at us girls."

"What did he look like?" Paul Temple asked.

Betty closed her eyes in an effort to remember. She wasn't very good at describing people. "He was about sixty, I suppose. Almost as tall as me, and he smiled the whole time. Perhaps he was just good natured. Oh yes, and he had a northern accent."

When they dropped her off at the end of her road it was gone half past one and Betty Stanway was worried again. Not as worried as she had been, because Paul Temple had promised her there would be no unpleasantness, no publicity. He had a friend at Scotland Yard called Charlie Vosper who was a very nice man, and Charlie Vosper would come and see her on Monday when she was back in London. But it didn't seem right.

"I know you'll probably think I'm crazy," she had said as she got out of the car. "But in spite of what's happened, with Des walking out on me, I'm still very fond of him."

Paul Temple's smile was warmly reassuring, and then the Rolls drove on. She watched it out of sight before walking the last fifty yards to the house where she had spent her childhood.

The semi-detached houses were all in darkness and they all looked strangely the same to her now. She deliberately tried to feel her way back to the girl who had known every kid in the street, who had belonged among these gardens and homes and the footpaths at the back, a securely happy and slightly reckless Betty Stanway.

There was somebody standing by her front gate. She could only see the shadow in the dark until she was close to him, and then she stopped in amazement.

"Why," she said, and her voice sounded more frightened than amazed, "Des!"

CHAPTER 4

THEY were across the borders into Worcestershire and even in the dark Paul could feel the difference in the countryside, sense the hills and smell the fields. In his more ecstatic moments, such as when they had bought Random Cottage a few years ago, Paul described Broadway literally as the heart of England. Whenever he arrived there for a few days snatched from London life he wanted to give up the metropolis and become a country gentleman. But he usually found that his novels were progressing too slowly in the country. The pace was too slow, and an innate puritanism would drive him back again to the rat race. However, for the next week or so Paul knew he would be totally content.

Going for walks through the wooded hills, a few hours writing in the afternoon, down to the village pub of an evening for a gossip, catching up on his reading. Being with Steve. What more can life afford?

"Do you think that Desmond whatever-his-name-is could be one of your criminal master minds?" Steve asked.

"Eh? No." They were driving through the village and Paul switched on the full headlamps to catch the turning into their lane past the war memorial. "Darling, there have always been master minds in crime. I said that the new master minds are not the criminal type. They come from the new meritocracy. I know even that is not very original, but it's less corny than you make it sound. It happens to be true."

His new novel was going to be a character study of a brilliant scholarship lad from Salford, the same generation as Mary Quant and Jim Slater, an entrepreneur who applies all his originality to a career in crime. Paul was toying with the idea of calling his hero Jonathan Wild.

"She was certainly an attractive girl."

"Who?" asked Paul.

"Betty Stanway. I wonder what made him stand her up."

"Oh. Yes."

"She seemed a little uncertain of herself, as if she thought being a dancer wasn't quite respectable. She thought she had thrown herself at Desmond Blane." Steve laughed with unladylike glee. "She should have seen me hurl myself at you!"

Paul was hurt. "I won you by stealth, madam. You've no idea how I plotted—"

It was a narrow lane and Random Cottage was a hundred yards along, shielded by trees and lying back in the grounds. Paul jumped from the car and opened the gates. He was wondering whether he would find time to clear the undergrowth of what he ironically described as the garden when he realised there was a dog barking nearby.

"What is it?" Steve called from the car.

"I don't know. Listen."

The dog was barking and howling continuously.

"Perhaps it's from the farm," said Steve. "The wind is blowing in this direction."

"Perhaps."

Steve turned into the driveway and ran the car down to the garage. Paul closed the gates behind her and followed on foot. The barking grew louder.

"Paul! It's coming from the garage."

The dog was obviously hurling itself against the garage door in some distress. Paul unlocked the doors and pulled them open. A wire haired fox terrier hurtled into the drive. Its tone changed to delighted yapping as it jumped up at Paul in friendly welcome.

"Steady boy," Paul said cautiously, "you've got muddy paws."

"What's he doing here?" Steve asked.

"I can't imagine." He tried to hold the dog long enough to examine its collar, but this was taken to be a game and the dog bounded off along the drive, barked happily at the Rolls and scurried round again to Paul. "Will you hold him, Steve, while I take a look at his collar?"

She was laughing so much that the frightened dog vanished beneath the car. Eventually Paul dragged it out in front of the headlights. It had a brass identity disc.

"Well?" Steve asked.

"It says, Gavin Renson, Harkdale 892304."

"Renson?" Steve stood up. "That was one of the names Desmond Blane mentioned in his telephone call. Skibby and Renson. I'm certain Betty Stanway said Renson."

Paul was looking at his hands. Then he turned the dog round as if he were examining it for injury.

"What is it, Paul?"

"This isn't mud on the dog, Steve. I think it's blood. And the dog is not injured."

The car's headlamps were shining directly into the garage, but Paul had been too preoccupied with the dog to notice what looked like a bundle of old clothes in the far corner. He went into the garage and switched on the main lights.

"Stay where you are, Steve."

The garage was big enough for two large cars and it also accommodated a work bench and space for engineering feats. Paul went across to the bundle half concealed beneath the work bench. It was the body of a young man. When Paul turned it over he found the side of the young man's head had been beaten in. A heavy tyre lever beside him looked the obvious murder weapon.

"So this is Gavin Renson," he murmured.

The fox terrier sniffed its master and wagged its tail rather tentatively.

"You've no idea who Blane was talking to when he mentioned the name Renson?"

Paul had sighed wearily. "No, I'm sorry, I haven't, Inspector. I asked Betty who it was and she said she didn't know."

The inspector had puffed with dubious concentration at his pipe. "Do you think she was telling the truth, or was she covering up for her boyfriend?"

"I think she was telling the truth." Paul had shrugged helplessly. "After all, she needn't have told me the story in the first place if she hadn't wanted to."

"No, I suppose not."

It had been three o'clock when they got to bed, and Paul slept badly. He felt slightly outraged at finding a corpse in his country retreat. This was the kind of thing which happened to other people, and of his own free will he sometimes became involved in murder cases in London. But Broadway was away from it all. This was an intrusion!

Twice Paul got up in the night to make a cup of coffee. He could understand the girl coming to him with her story, because he had mentioned Harkdale and they had been on television in the same programme. It was natural. But why had Renson been battered to death in his garage? That was a little calculated of someone. Only why? The second time he got up Paul watched the dawn creep through the valley below the cottage. The cold grey light touched Bredon Hill and then moved visibly across the brown trees and into the fields. There were no greens or yellows in the coming of day, no warmth. Paul went back to bed, huddled against Steve's soft body and fell deeply asleep.

"You say you'd never heard of Gavin Renson?"

"No," said Paul, "I hadn't."

"You haven't the slightest idea, in fact, what he was doing here?"

"Not the slightest."

The bedroom faced east towards Snowshill and at nine o'clock a low sun was shining through the window into his face. He was half woken by the unfamiliar din of a dog chasing something through the bushes at the side of the house.

"But you've seen this before, I take it?" The police inspector pointed to the tyre lever.

"Of course. It belongs to me."

"Have you ever used it?"

"Yes, I can change a tyre." Paul felt rather defensive about it. "I'm an intellectual, Inspector, so I take a pride in my ability to tinker with cars, potter knowledgeably in the garden and do jobs around the house. I enjoy surprising myself."

"Have you used it recently?"

Paul tried to shield his eyes from the blinding, interrogating light. "No, I've been in London." He blinked rapidly and realised that he was awake. Steve had drawn the curtains and was standing by the bed with his morning coffee. She had clearly been up some time.

"I've been dreaming about that inspector," he grumbled. "Going over and over in my mind—"

"He's downstairs again."

"Oh God." He yawned and glanced at the clock by the bed. "He only left here six hours ago. Doesn't he have a home and a loving wife?"

Steve laughed. "Yes, and I think he blames you for keeping him from them."

"I don't believe the loving wife part."

Paul took his time over coffee, had a leisurely bath and dressed with slow deliberation. It was more like early summer now. The rooks were quarrelling among themselves in the elm trees and across the fields a tractor was chugging about its work. Paul enjoyed the sounds of the country. He opened a window and filled his London lungs with the smell of the Cotswolds. Then he went downstairs to breakfast.

Luckily Inspector Manley was out in the garage with his squad of investigators; they were looking for fingerprints and searching for things they may have missed in the middle of the night. Paul ate his cornflakes in the two minutes fifty seconds it took to boil his egg.

"What sort of questions has he been asking?" Paul asked.

"About our country habits," Steve laughed. "He can't get it into his head that we aren't weekenders. I've told him that we come down here as and when we feel like it. But he thinks you ought to have a proper job with regular working hours."

Paul grunted. "I do have. I'm supposed to be starting work on my novel this morning."

"That doesn't count with Inspector Manley. He thinks there's something almost unemployed about you."

The fox terrier bounded into the kitchen to welcome Paul, barked a couple of warning threats at a policeman in the drive and then attacked the chocolate biscuits Steve had put down for him. "He wouldn't eat the digestives," she explained.

Inspector Manley was from Birmingham C.I.D. and if there was one thing he distrusted more than a man without a regular job it was a Londoner. He was phlegmatic, smoked a pipe and spoke with an unidentifiable regional accent. A square set man in his late fifties who appeared to work on the principle that if he worried away at a case long enough it would solve itself. His square head was perched neckless on broad shoulders. He came into the kitchen at the marmalade and toast stage.

"Coffee, Inspector?" Steve asked with natural friendliness.

"Thanks." He sat at the table and looked suspiciously at Paul. "So you're up then? I've just heard from the doctor.

Renson was killed between eight and eleven last night."

"I was at the television studios."

"I know." He glowered. "That's a funny way to pass the time."

Paul agreed. "But it's better than spending the evening watching television."

"You must have a lot of money," he said. "A house like this, a mews house in London, running a Rolls."

"And me," Steve said.

"Very expensive."

Paul explained that he worked extremely hard, but the inspector looked sceptical. He wasn't even impressed when Paul said that while he was writing a novel he worked sixteen hours a day.

"I've been working sixteen hours a day on this series of bank robberies, Mr. Temple."

"I hope you're getting somewhere."

"We have been since the Harkdale robbery. For the past forty-eight hours, believe it or not, we've been trying to find this man Gavin Renson. We've been trying to find him because it's our belief the money was handed over to Renson within ten minutes of the raid taking place."

"What do you mean, handed over?" Paul asked. "Where was Renson?"

"There's a lay-by this side of Harkdale; quite a large one, near a wood. You've probably passed it many times."

"Between Harkdale and Lower Winfield?"

"That's right. On the day of the robbery Renson was waiting there with a lorry. Immediately after the raid Skibby and company belted past the lay-by and—" His square face almost grinned. "I'm sure I don't have to tell you what happened, Mr. Temple."

"They threw Renson the bag?"

Inspector Manley nodded.

"Was Renson alone?"

"Yes." The inspector glanced down at the dog. "Except for Jackson, of course. They sell special biscuits for dogs, you know." The dog wagged its tail as it heard its name.

"Is his name Jackson?" asked Steve. "It's a curious name for a dog."

"It is indeed, Mrs. Temple. According to our reports Renson thought the world of him. Absolutely devoted. But I must say the dog doesn't look too put out by the death of his master."

Paul glanced at his watch. It was gone ten. Time to go upstairs and lock himself in the study before Mrs. O'Hanrahan arrived. She was due at ten. The study was one of those attic conversions in pine and glass. Paul claimed a little recklessly that he could see six counties through the huge panoramic window.

"Will you be needing me for a few hours, Inspector?" he asked. "I have work to do."

"I don't know. My men are searching just in case Renson brought the money here with him. I'll be hanging around." He puffed gloomily on his pipe. "There isn't much else to do. Renson was our big break, and the trail stops here."

"What about Desmond Blane? Shouldn't you be—?"

"We've put out a call. But Blane is a London man."

Paul laughed. Obviously Inspector Manley had been busily hunting for a gang based in Birmingham which had been making the forays into the surrounding countryside. It was a blow to him that the gang might operate from the smoke.

"I expect my old friend Charlie Vosper of the Yard will be able to help you," Paul said cruelly.

"Which yard?"

He had left it too late. Paul heard the front door slam and a woman's voice yelled, "Yoo hoo! Anyone at home?" To flee upstairs he would have to pass her in the passage.

"She's our daily woman," Paul told the inspector. "Mrs.

O'Hanrahan."

"I didn't know you had a daily woman."

Paul nodded, picked up *The Times* from the floor and tried to become absorbed in it. He looked up the two answers he had failed to get in the crossword yesterday, and found he couldn't remember the clues.

"Would she have been here yesterday?" the inspector asked.

Steve nodded. "She would have opened up. You know, cleaned through and made the beds, turned on the heating. Mrs. O'Hanrahan is very conscientious."

Mrs. O'Hanrahan had a heart of gold and a very loud voice. She was a large all-enveloping woman in her fifties. She had survived three husbands and she terrorised the elderly bachelors in the village pub. After three stouts she was anybody's. When Paul and Steve had bought Random Cottage it had been she, Mrs. O'Hanrahan, who had decided they would need someone to keep an eye on the place while they were in London. And Mrs. O'Hanrahan had soon afterwards decided that Steve was too much of a lady to cope with all the housework. Actually Steve was very fond of her.

"There you are, the two of you. Have you seen the police outside? Mrs. T., you're looking frail. You need the country air in your lungs. It's all right, I know that Mr. T. is fit as a parish priest. I saw you on the telly last night and you looked as real as my late husband."

"I'm real," Paul muttered, "and I'm alive."

"God bless you. I nearly fell off the bar stool when you mentioned Harkdale. You must be psychic after all. We had a man here yesterday wanting to talk to you about the Harkdale robbery. Ever such a nice young man." She paused in surprise. "That's his dog under the sink."

She went across and made a fuss of the animal. She clearly regarded Random Cottage as hers and Paul and Steve as a couple of her responsibilities. Steve was a sweet and innocent girl who only needed fattening up; Paul was more complex but she understood his funny ways.

"What are all these policemen doing here?" she asked suddenly.

"The nice young man has been murdered," Paul said.

Mrs. O'Hanrahan sat quickly in the armchair by the kitchen range. "Lord almighty." She clutched her bosom and accepted a cup of coffee from Steve.

"I'm Inspector Manley of Birmingham C.I.D. and I'm investigating the death of Gavin Renson. Did he say why he wanted to see Mr. Temple yesterday?"

"No, he said he had read a series of articles in some newspaper or other. Of course Mr. Temple wasn't due here until midnight—"

"What time did Renson arrive?"

"He came to the front door at about three o'clock. I was just off myself because it had been a busy day—"

"Did you see him leave?"

"Yes. He said he'd come back this morning."

Paul folded *The Times* and tucked it under his arm. He gestured to Steve and the inspector that he was off upstairs to do some work, but they didn't notice. He went upstairs into the study. It was an imposing room, like the office of an American tycoon, with a luxury desk in the modern idiom, spacious bookshelves, an incomprehensible punched card filing system, chairs and pictures and a battery of gadgets.

He flicked the switch of his telephone answering gadget and listened to the crop of insignificant messages. While messages were being played back Paul stared out of the panoramic window. He suspected he used to work better in his tiny basement office ten years or more ago. The rolling English countryside was distracting.

He sat at the desk and pushed away his electric typewriter.

Paul began making notes with a fountain pen on his note pad. What sort of person would be a super-brain of criminal organisation? Would it show at school, or at university? Would class enter into it, as a determining factor in the decision between banking and bank robbery? Would age enter into it? Was a criminal's most creative period finished, like a logician's, by the time he was thirty? Was crime an art or a craft or a science? Paul stared at the questions before him, and found that he was thinking about something else. Instead of looking for answers he was wondering about Betty Stanway. Oh well, it amounted to the same thing. He might as well find out who was behind the series of bank robberies. See whether he was young or old, grammar school or comprehensive, creative or thorough.

Paul picked up the telephone, asked for directory enquiries, and gave them the name of Stanway and the street he had left Betty in.

"Hello, caller," the operator said impersonally. "The subscriber is a Mr. Christopher Stanway, he's listed as a dentist. The number is Oxford 09037."

"Thank you, operator," said Paul.

He dialled the number.

"Good morning, Mr. Stanway. I wonder whether I could speak to your daughter Betty. My name is Temple."

"Who? Betty? She isn't here." The voice on the other end of the line was triumphant. It was Betty's younger brother, Pete, and he wanted to know who Temple was. "Well, I'm afraid my sister lives in London. We almost never see her."

"But she is staying with you at the moment," Paul said patiently. "I dropped her off at the end of your road last night."

"Sorry, but she didn't come at the last moment. She rang to say that she'd been held up. Try the Love-Inn, or alternatively try the next name on your list of prospects."

The young man hung up. Paul replaced the receiver. He was suddenly worried. He hurried downstairs to find Inspector Manley still in the kitchen.

"Inspector, I've just been onto Betty Stanway's home. She never arrived there last night!"

"I know." The inspector puffed at his pipe and sighed. "That has been worrying me."

"But we dropped her at the corner of the street," said Steve in amazement, "just near her house!"

Paul nodded. "She didn't make the last fifty yards."

"It's like I was saying to the inspector," declared Mrs. O'Hanrahan, "it's all very mysterious!"

Paul glared at her. "Inspector Manley, the girl apparently telephoned to say that she had been held up. Do you know where she telephoned from?"

"Her father thought London, but he couldn't be certain."

"Perhaps," said Steve, "she went back to London because she'd forgotten something."

The inspector shook his phlegmatic head. "We've spoken to her landlady. She hasn't gone back to her flat."

Paul thought for a moment and then said, "I'm going back to Town."

"Don't worry, Mr. Temple, I'll look after Steve—"

Paul smiled weakly at Mrs. O'Hanrahan and went through into the living room. He gathered together the papers he might need. While he was deciding whether or not to ring Kate Balfour and warn her that he would be coming the inspector wandered into the room.

"May I come in?" he asked.

"Yes, of course, Inspector."

Manley leaned against the door and sighed. "According to Mrs. O'Hanrahan, this man Renson came here to talk to you about the Harkdale robbery. I wonder why."

"Yes, Inspector, I wonder why. Do you suppose the thieves

are falling out? How much money was involved? I've seen various sums mentioned in the press."

"Forty-two thousand pounds," he said sourly. "But this was the fifth robbery in the series. There's big money involved."

Paul grunted. He went upstairs to the study, and the inspector followed him. The inspector looked disapprovingly at all the books and papers.

"Of course, he may simply have lost his nerve," said Paul. "With three of his colleagues dead and a policeman killed, he may have got scared."

"I would understand that," said the inspector. "I can see that a simple minded crook might get scared when he finds himself in the big time. But what I still don't understand is you, Mr. Temple. Why did he come and see you?"

Paul smiled non-committally. He wished he knew.

"By the way, Inspector, if anything develops, or if you want me for anything, give me a ring. You should have my number at the station."

"I will."

"I'll be back here sometime tomorrow."

Downstairs in the kitchen Mrs. O'Hanrahan was playing with the dog. The game consisted of chasing it and throwing one of Paul's best slippers across the room. Steve was laughing delightedly.

"Darling," she said as the dog cannoned against Paul's legs, "what are we going to do about Jackson?"

"What do you mean?" Paul tried to retrieve his slipper without appearing to be a spoilsport, but the dog thought he was joining in the fun. "He isn't our responsibility."

"I know he isn't." Steve was tentative. "I just wondered what was going to happen to him."

"We'll talk about Jackson later."

"Yes, darling." She kissed him on the cheek. "Are you off now?"

The car was still in the drive. Paul tossed his briefcase into the passenger seat and opened the door. He wondered whether the dog could be trained to frighten off undesirable visitors, like burglars or Mrs. O'Hanrahan.

"By the way, Inspector," he said suddenly. "Forty-two thousand pounds is a lot of money for a small bank in Harkdale. Were the robbers tipped off by someone with inside knowledge?"

"We think so, but at the moment we haven't a clue who it was." He slammed the door after Paul had climbed into the car. "The money only arrived at Harkdale the night before, and it was due for distribution the following afternoon."

Paul started up the engine and then waited for Steve to catch the dog from somewhere under the rear wheels. He laughed. Perhaps London was the most peaceful place to be after all.

CHAPTER 5

"BETTY STANWAY? I don't know what you think she's been up to, Mr. Temple, but I can assure you that she is an extremely respectable girl. I'm afraid I can't help you."

Paul smiled his most reassuring smile. "I know, Mrs. Garnett, she's a very nice girl, but she's in trouble. I'm trying to help her. Perhaps I could have a word with you?"

It was many years since Paul had lived in conflict with landladies, yet somewhere in his stomach there was a twinge of apprehension. The breed didn't change. She stood in the doorway of the Belsize Park Gardens house like a symbol of morality in the face of lust and late night parties and men.

"Betty doesn't live here any more."

"She's in trouble," Paul repeated. "She's young and in love and it's up to us to help her. We are mature and responsible people."

It worked. "I told her not to fall in love with that man of hers, but she wouldn't listen. She was getting ideas in that night club where she worked. It turned her head." She showed Paul down the steps into the basement of the house. "This is where Betty lived. She was an attractive girl, and London is hard on attractive girls. I should know."

"Really?" Paul asked in polite surprise.

"She thought I was only her landlady, as if spoiling a girl's fun comes naturally to landladies. But I know what it's like. I arrived in London with only my looks to show for it and I was swept off my feet by a charming layabout."

"You say she doesn't live here any more?" Paul asked.

"Mr. Garnett paid for this house, but he never earned a penny more than he could spend on booze while he was alive. He dreamed of easy money and a comfortable life, but the most profitable thing he ever did was to get run over one night at closing time. I bought this house with the insurance money."

"Did she give in her notice?" asked Paul.

"Who?"

"Betty Stanway." Her furnished flat was two rooms, a bedroom and a kitchen. Her possessions were still in place. The vast range of clothes and a dressing table piled with cosmetics. It was difficult to form an impression of the girl through the muddle. A Degas reproduction on the wall, a few books by Noel Streatfeild and Angela Thirkell. "When did she leave here?"

"She called in this afternoon. Paid me a week's rent in lieu of notice and said that she would send for her things."

"Who was with her?"

"Nobody. She was by herself." The woman was nearly sixty, a bird of prey with a hooked nose and an eagle eye for trouble. "What is Betty doing, Mr. Temple?"

"I don't know. Did she tell you where she was going?"

"No. She said she was off to the club." The woman sat on the edge of Betty's unmade bed and shook her head forebodingly. "Betty was a funny girl. I think she was probably romantic, lived in a dream world out of her children's books. She was usually unhappy."

"You must have known her very well," said Paul.

Mrs. Garnett smiled with sinister indulgence. "Somebody had to look after her, and I must admit that I tried. She used to come home at all hours, but of course that was part of her job. She used to drink quite a lot, but those men at the club have to pay for it. It wasn't a life that could go on forever. I suppose she didn't know how to change it and settle down. She didn't have many friends."

Paul left the house feeling slightly sad for the girl. The bed-sit life was fun for a couple of years when you were twenty, but Betty had been too old for it and she had seen defeat coming. He hoped she wasn't too desperate. Wherever she was.

"Why," Paul asked his favourite barman, "why would a gang of bank robbers try to involve an attractive dancer in their activities?"

Eric polished a few glasses and served a sporty type with a half of bitter while he thought about it. "Search me, Mr. T.," he said at last. "What's the answer?"

"I don't know."

"Perhaps they like having attractive dancers about the place."

Paul sipped his whisky and stared at his reflection in the mirror behind the bar. It could be, of course, simply that Desmond Blane always took three weeks to make up his mind.

"I'm going to the Love-Inn to find out," said Paul.

"I'll come with you," said Eric. "I'm off duty in ten minutes."

"That would help with the parking," Paul said discouragingly.

He telephoned the Love-Inn and asked for Rita Fletcher. He explained that he was worried about Betty Stanway and wanted to come and see her.

"Betty?" the woman asked cheerfully. "The police have been here asking questions, but I'm not aware that anything is wrong. Betty is due here this evening, and as far as I know she'll be turning up as usual." There was a pause, and she added, "But come and see me by all means. I have been worried recently about Betty."

Eric Jordan was usually infallible about the London scene, but he couldn't tell Paul much about the Love-Inn. It was owned by some American who had never yet ventured into any other business. It was run by a dynamic woman. It was run well and had never been raided by the police. It was just another club, with no known criminal connections.

"What time shall I pick you up, Mr. T.?"

"Yes," said Paul, "that's a good question."

"I could always come in with you if you wanted. Just in case you find what you're looking for."

It was half past ten in the evening and the streets of Soho were still thronged with people in search of the permissive society. The dark narrow streets with their glitter of neon and aura of naughtiness, the furtive figures in doorways, all contributed to the feeling Eric Jordan obviously had that he was missing out on something. He had agreed instantly to chauffeur Paul into the West End, and now he was visibly reluctant to leave.

"I'd like to see what the other half look like," he murmured sadly.

"This is business," said Paul. "You'd better give me an hour. I'll see you here at eleven thirty."

He got out of the car and glanced up at the flashing sign which announced The Love-Inn. There were photographs of The Melody Girls in the open foyer, startlingly pink and jolly, revealing enough flesh to belie the claim, 'As seen on TV'. There were photographs of male crooners in evening dress who had been popular fifteen years ago, and there was a series of portraits of a strip tease dancer labelled teasingly, 'Now Showing'. Paul turned apologetically to Eric Jordan.

Eric was nodding amiably at a young man who was going into the Love-Inn. He was a fair, sharply dressed young man and Paul caught a whiff of hair lotion as he passed. Eric grinned.

The young man went through a door marked Private which clearly led back stage, so Paul followed him. The noise of the orchestra was brashly close at hand and it sounded as if something unpleasant was happening on stage. The soaring trumpet was ecstatic, and from the reaction of the saxophones and drummer you would never think the musicians had seen it all before. There were show girls wandering unconcerned along the corridor, and stage hands were pushing past in readiness to strike sets and wheel on props as if they had seen it all before and forgotten what it was.

"Hey, you!" An aged stage door keeper was leaning out of his cubby hole at the end of the corridor waving at Paul. "How did you get in here? Yes, you!"

Paul pushed through to the man. "I want to see Miss Fletcher. She is expecting me."

"Oh yes?" he said disbelievingly. "What name?"

"Paul Temple." The fair haired friend of Eric's appeared from one of the dressing rooms with a tall chorus girl. Paul gave the stage door keeper a ten shilling piece. "I telephoned about an hour ago."

"You'd better wait in her office. It's more comfortable in there." He grinned toothlessly and pocketed the money. I'll tell her you've arrived."

The office was a converted dressing room, but the expensive furniture and the well stocked drinks cabinet indicated that Rita Fletcher was doing very nicely. A wall of photographs to My Darling Rita indicated that all the best show-biz people recognised her success.

"By the way," said Paul, "who was that young man we just passed in the corridor? Fair haired young chap with wandering hands."

"Him? Name of Sampson." The stage door keeper scratched his behind in disapproval. "A proper bleedin' twit he is. I don't know why Mr. Coley lets him hang about here all the time." He hitched up his trousers. "I'll tell Miss Fletcher."

Paul sat in a deep leather armchair and lit a cigarette. Somewhere in the distance he could hear the applause of the audience and there was a renewed flurry of activity in the corridor. Then the door opened and a short man in a dinner jacket came in. He had an empty glass in his hand and he moved across the office to the drinks cabinet as if he knew his way about. But he stopped abruptly as he saw Paul.

"Hi," he said.

"Good evening," said Paul. "My name's Temple. I'm waiting for Miss Fletcher."

"Tam Coley," the man explained. "Glad to know you." He raised his glass in salute, then continued across to the cabinet to pour himself a large gin. "What did you say your name was?"

"Temple," said Paul.

Tam Coley nodded. "That's right. I know that name." He was an American and from his accent Paul placed him tentatively as a New Yorker, the Bronx rather than Brooklyn. "Heard the name before somewhere. Don't you write books or something?"

"Books," Paul said mildly. "What do you do, Mr. Coley?"

"I own this joint." He laughed at the improbability of it. "Say, wait a minute! You didn't come here to write a book?"

"No. I've just told you, I came to see Miss Fletcher."

Tam Coley looked slightly relieved, but he sipped his gin in silence. "Is Rita a friend of yours?" he asked doubtfully.

"No. I'm interested in a friend of hers, and I hoped she might put me in touch with him."

"Oh? Who's that?"

"A man called Desmond Blane."

Coley was relaxed again as he shook his head. "Never heard of him. Doesn't sound like a man, sounds more like a seaside resort. Bognor Regis, Desmond Blane, Ashby de la Zouche." He smiled at the empty glass. "Did you know, Mr. Temple, that Ashby de la Zouche is not by the seaside? The popular song has it all inaccurate!"

"Blane is a friend of Betty Stanway's," said Paul. "Now don't tell me you've never heard of Miss Stanway?"

"Sure I've heard of her. She works for me." He chuckled and filled his glass again. "Are you sure it isn't Miss Stanway you're interested in, eh, and not Mr. Blane?"

"I'm interested in both of them."

Paul had decided that the man was not a fool. He was a wiry little American, middle aged and amiably alcoholic, but he had enough shrewdness to move in on the ruthless London club scene. He probably traded on people taking him for a fool.

"What's going on, Temple?" he asked cautiously. "The police dropped in on the club this afternoon and they asked a whole lot of questions about Betty Stanway. How long had she been working here, they asked, when did we last see her, had she a regular boyfriend. Pretty pointless damned questions."

"If they asked so many questions," Paul intervened, "it's my guess they mentioned Mr. Blane."

Tam Coley blinked. "Come to think of it, I believe they did."

"I thought you hadn't heard of him?"

Coley suddenly grinned at him. "Say, you're bright! Very bright! I must read one of those books of yours."

The door opened and a buxom woman in her forties flounced in. A smartly fashionable woman with a frill too many and an air of determination. She glared at Tam Coley and stayed holding the door open.

"I thought you were out front," she said to him. "There's a football crowd out there and I'd like someone to keep an eye on the girls."

Tam Coley paddled cheerfully out with a nod to Paul, but he stopped as a thought occurred to him. "Oh, ah, has Betty arrived?" he asked.

"Yes, but she isn't staying. She wants to give in her notice—"

"You mean she has another job?"

Rita Fletcher spread out her hands in bewilderment. "I don't know, Tam. She probably isn't well."

"What's the matter with her?"

"Goodness knows, but leave her alone, Tam. Take it easy, will you?"

Coley stared at her for a moment. "Look, Rita, I don't know what that kid's been up to, but whatever it is I don't want any trouble. Right now this lousy dump has a highly respectable reputation, and I wanna keep it that way."

Rita nodded obediently. "There's nothing to worry about, Tam."

"I hope you're right. We don't get involved, remember that."

"Yes, Tam."

With the serious interlude completed Tam Coley turned back to Paul and grinned. "Nice meeting you, Mr.—er—?"

"Temple."

"Mr. Temple." He raised his glass in farewell and left.

Rita waited until he was safely away before slamming the door behind him.

"He's a boring little lush," she explained to Paul, "but he owns the place. I suppose he owns most of us who work here as well. Sit down, Mr. Temple. I'm sorry I kept you waiting."

She sat behind the desk. She gave an impression of irritable energy, but Paul assumed that was something to do with the football supporters. The energy, authority and mature good looks appealed to him. She was a successful woman.

"So you gave Betty a lift into Oxford yesterday," she said.

"That's right. And I'd like to know what happened to her after I dropped her off near her home."

"So would I." Rita Fletcher took a cigarette from the silver box on the desk, lit it and inhaled deeply. "I've been talking to her for twenty minutes and I can't get any sense out of her. She isn't interested. She wasn't even interested when I told her the police had been here asking questions." The woman's eyes met Paul's. "Is she in real trouble, Mr. Temple?"

"Perhaps. And her friend Desmond Blane is certainly in trouble. But I believe you know Mr. Blane. Didn't you introduce him to Betty?"

"Yes, I introduced him to Betty. But he isn't a friend of mine." She went restlessly across to the drinks cabinet and offered Paul a whisky. "There are hundreds of people like Desmond Blane who come to the club regularly. If they're wealthy we try to be nice to them." She handed Paul a glass.

"Thanks. Is Blane a wealthy man?"

Rita smiled cynically. "I thought he was, but now I'm not so sure. I was probably wrong."

Paul raised an enquiring eyebrow.

"He's disappeared," she continued, "and this afternoon the police hinted that he might have something to do with a series of bank robberies up in the Midlands. I don't mind that, the banks are there to dish out money when people need it, but I'd like to strangle him for upsetting one of my girls."

Paul laughed at the woman's indignation. "Are you fond of Betty?" he asked.

"Of course I'm fond of her. She's temperamental and difficult to handle, but she's a nice kid, which is more than you can say for most of the little bitches around here." She stubbed out the cigarette. "Do you want to talk with her?"

"Thanks." Paul finished his drink and stood up. "I only hope I'll be able to get through to her."

"Take her out and buy her a drink." Rita Fletcher's eyes flashed ironically at Paul. "She's susceptible to environment and charm, like the rest of us."

The dressing room had that smell of greasepaint which reminded Paul unhappily of the television chat show. But the Love-Inn didn't provide luxury for its employees; the room was obviously shared by three other girls and they all had a wall each, with their own mirror topped with a row of electric light bulbs. Betty Stanway's wall was no less tidy than the others. Her make-up was scattered over the table, among the cigarettes and ashtray and transistor radio and handbag. There was also an Aer-Lingus timetable beside an empty glass. But Betty Stanway wasn't there.

"She was here a few minutes ago," said Rita. "I'll see if she's next door."

While Rita was next door Paul glanced at the Aer-Lingus timetable. He let it fall open at random, on the principle that it would open where it had been most read. It opened at Dublin. Paul didn't have much faith in that as a scientific method, but it was interesting. He was even more interested in the book of matches by the girl's ashtray. They were from The Gateway Motel, Banbury, according to the cover. Paul slipped the matches into his pocket.

"She's not in any of the other dressing rooms," said Rita as she came back. "But she must be in the club still because her handbag is here."

Paul sat on the visitors' sofa by the wardrobe of flimsy costumes and said he would wait. A fan dancer's feathers tickled his ear. He hoped that Betty would return before the other three girls came in to change. He could imagine the four girls destroying all his illusions of feminine mystery.

There was another rumble of applause from the distance. Paul stood up and gestured towards the door. "Maybe we should—"

At that moment Betty Stanway came into the dressing room. She was wearing the same trim green outfit she had been wearing when Paul had picked her up outside the Television Studios. She looked unwelcoming and worried.

"We've been looking for you," said Rita.

"I was out front," she said distantly. "Tam wanted to see me."

"I told him to leave you alone."

The girl shrugged. "He was worried about the police."

"Don't take any notice of him, Betty. He'll be paralytic in a couple of hours." She smiled encouragingly at Paul. "I'll leave you two alone, shall I? I'll be in my office if I'm needed."

Betty picked up the handbag from her table and handed it to Rita. "You left this behind."

Rita Fletcher laughed and said she was becoming more like Tam Coley every day. Then she went. In the silence she left behind her Betty Stanway waited defiantly.

"I suppose you want to talk about last night?"

"That's up to you Betty—"

"Well, it's none of your damned business!"

"What about discussing this somewhere else?" Paul asked. "Have you eaten? Do you fancy a drink?"

She thawed slightly and asked what Steve would say.

"She'll be very jealous."

That was good enough for Betty, and they went round to the club bar. "But I shan't tell you anything," she warned. It was sufficient, usually, to have a drink with the girl. Men didn't expect her to talk. So she had a sweet martini and listened to Paul. It was her usual role.

The club bar was at the back of the auditorium, so that the thirstier customers could get a drink without missing a nipple. It meant that the absorbed men in the rear rows shouted angrily if you asked for a double whisky too loudly, and normal communication was difficult. As Paul spoke he could hear one of the girls on stage suddenly call to a man in the front row, "Don't get too carried away, buster!"

A few moments later the bouncer escorted a shamefaced man from the auditorium. Paul wondered what he had been doing. He looked like an average office clerk with a small wife and a small family car.

"Why does all this matter so much to you?" Betty asked

sulkily.

"I'm not accustomed to finding bodies in the garage, not in Broadway. That's where I go to get away from it all. And of course Steve was a little put out. You know how squeamish women are." It occurred to Paul as he was talking that Steve had taken it in her stride. Perhaps being married to him was making her callous. "The interesting aspect was that the man's name was Gavin Renson. You remember—"

"Yes, I read about his death in the paper."

"Renson was one of the names you mentioned last night. Your friend Desmond Blane—"

She shook her head.

"Gavin Renson was definitely mixed up in the Harkdale robbery!"

She didn't seem to be paying much attention. The Melody Girls were on stage in a fast and sinuous routine that had riveted the audience. Betty Stanway's fingers were tapping the top of the bar as if mentally she were up there going through all the movements with them.

"You remember the robbery?" Paul asked sarcastically.

She shook her head and smiled.

"Perhaps you don't remember the story you told me last night?" Paul was becoming exasperated. "Do you remember that I gave you a lift out to Oxford?"

Her eyes had strayed to the stage again. "My mother always warned me against accepting lifts from strangers."

"You asked me to help you last night, Betty, and I'm trying to help. I don't want to find your corpse next. Please, you must tell me what happened last night."

"I changed my mind." She spoke in the flat tones of somebody who couldn't be bothered to lie convincingly. "I never have got on with my father. So I went to stay with a girlfriend."

"Which girlfriend?"

"You wouldn't know her."

Paul was suddenly angry. He told her that he had given her story to the police and his voice was louder than it should have been. A couple of connoisseurs turned round to stare. "The police won't believe this foolish story about a girlfriend," he concluded in a whisper.

"So what?" she sighed. "Why should I worry?"

The audience were applauding, and close at hand it sounded no louder than it had from the dressing rooms. One of the ancient crooners was due on next. Paul glanced at his watch and wondered whether he could bear the memories. He would rather go home.

"Shall I tell you what I think happened?" he said in a final effort. "I think Blane was waiting for you last night. He picked you up and you went off together."

"No," she murmured.

"I think he is using you in some way, and before you realise it you'll be involved in the whole series of bank robberies. And then God help you!" He stood up and prepared to leave. The crooner was already receiving his nostalgic welcome.

"I haven't seen Desmond for nearly a month—"

"No? Then what would have induced you to give up your job here? You're not an adventurous girl, Betty, you wouldn't have thought of it yourself. I know it's grim to be dancing in a club all your life, but what will your alternative lead to?"

Betty looked disenchantedly around the club.

"What are your plans?" Paul asked.

"To give up dancing."

"I noticed the Aer Lingus timetable on your dressing table. Are you going away with Des, or running away from him?"

"Does it matter?" She pouted apologetically. "I know what I'm doing, and it's my life—"

Paul cut in impatiently. "If you change your mind, Betty, give me a ring. But don't leave it too late."

He left her sitting helplessly at the bar. She wouldn't be helped. Paul walked quickly through the foyer; she looked quite different in the publicity photographs, pinker and more intelligent. Paul looked along the street for Eric Jordan. It was exactly half past eleven.

"How's that for timing?" Eric called. The Mini-Cooper drew up by his feet. "Hop in, Mr. T."

Paul slipped in gracefully. The streets as they drove away were still crowded and the flashing coloured lights dazzled with the promise of fun. The traffic jammed and drivers urgent for nameless destinations hooted and jaywalkers scampered through to their tubes and buses. Paul watched them thoughtfully. He began to relax as they drove down Whitehall and into Pimlico where the empty streets were in darkness.

"When you dropped me off tonight, Eric, you acknowledged a fair haired young man in a dark suit."

"Did I?" Eric remembered. "Yes, that's right."

"Is he a friend of yours?"

Eric laughed. "I wish he was. I could do with some friends in the right places. He used to work in my bank, but he seems to have left now. I've got another one of those girls who looks at me as if I was overdrawn—"

"His name is Sampson."

"Is it?" Eric said politely. "I didn't know his name. He just sat behind the counter and gave me my money or called the manager. I expect he's moved on to better things."

Eric prattled on about his instinctive fear of bank managers and the hard faced men of Wall Street until they reached the familiar streets of Chelsea. Civilisation, and home to an empty bed.

Paul had a nightcap before he went upstairs. He sat and watched the late night news on television. There was one sentence, among the items about politicians and distant wars and local demonstrations, which referred to the Harkdale robbery. It said that the legless man who had been identified as Ray Norton had recovered consciousness in hospital but he had been unable to help the police with their enquiries.

The lonely horror of the little crook's life struck Paul as so bleak that he had another drink. It was a long time since he had lived alone, and he had probably forgotten how to enjoy it. He undressed, washed, cleaned his teeth, and wondered what Steve was doing. He climbed into bed and scribbled a few notes on a pad.

"This gang," he noted, "cannot have suddenly come together fully formed. Whose gang, and what happened? Was their leader deposed by the new young whizz kid?"

CHAPTER 6

PAUL arrived back in Broadway at eleven o'clock next morning. He found Steve in the garden laying fertiliser beneath the rose bushes, while the dog yapped around her chasing butterflies. There was an early summer sun which picked out the yellow limestone of the cottage to perfection. It was all a little too much like an advertisement for something English.

"That dog will have to go," Paul called from the drive. "He looks as if you've hired him to complete the scene."

Steve wiped her brow and waved. "You're back early!"

"I had a quick breakfast with Inspector Vosper and then away." He crossed the lawn to bestow a kiss of approval. "Do you think those roses will bloom this year?"

"I doubt it, the soil isn't suitable." She dropped the trowel onto the pale green grass. "As a matter of fact I've been talking about the dog to Mrs. O'Hanrahan. She and Jackson have rather taken to each other, and she says that when we're not staying here she could very easily take care of him."

Paul looked suitably gratified. "We'll talk about the dog later, darling. Don't let me interrupt your gardening."

He went through into the kitchen, but Mrs. O'Hanrahan was sitting there enjoying her elevenses. Paul muttered hello and fled upstairs. At least Inspector Manley had left. He shut himself in the study and tried to continue the logical analysis he had been making during the journey.

Paul pinned a map of the Cotswolds and surrounding area on the makeshift noticeboard beside his desk. The map extended beyond Stratford and Worcester to the urban sprawl where Birmingham began. Paul stuck three coloured pins in it, to mark Aston Prior, Banham, and Harkdale. They didn't make much of a pattern, but they were close together. And they were all villages where the size of the bank had outgrown the local police force.

A certain local knowledge was indicated. Inspector Manley had said that the robbers had been tipped off from the inside. Presumably in all three cases. Paul noted three questions which needed answering. He was always surprised when a robbery done with inside help remained unsolved, because that indicated that the first man whom the thieves approached had co-operated. But surely the thieves would have to approach several people before finding a willing ear, so why do none of those several people speak? Paul noted a possible answer.

He wondered idly whether a better pattern would emerge from the map if they robbed another bank next Friday, but of course that was impossible. Of the three heavies who actually carried out the raids, two had been killed in the car crash and the third was still in hospital hovering legless between death and misery. This series of bank robberies was finished.

Immediate action was called for. The gang would be dispersing soon with the money. The four members whom Paul assumed to remain, with Betty Stanway as a possible fifth. He went downstairs and asked Mrs. O'Hanrahan to make some sandwiches.

"Steve!" he called. "Let's have lunch in the country. It's far too pleasant a day to skulk indoors."

"I'm not skulking indoors—"

"We'll drive out to Aston Prior. There's a marvellous little pub there which I've been meaning to visit. Picnic lunch—"

It was flat, dusty country raked with winds from the Bristol Channel. As the road dropped past Elmley Castle Paul felt as always that he was entering the Valley of Humiliation, and the image would be underlined fifteen or twenty miles later by the great smoking chimney stacks on the horizon. The Celestial City, he thought ironically. That was where the bank robbers had been heading, before they crashed.

Paul went over the gang in his mind; there had been two men in the car with Skibby Thorne: Larry Phillips and Ray Norton. As they had escaped they had thrown the money to Gavin Renson, which made them decoys. The brain behind these robberies obviously considered crooks to be disposable. That left Desmond Blane and perhaps his only recorded friend. Betty had said his name was Arnold something or other, about sixty, quite tall, with a northern accent. Blane and his friend had probably murdered Gavin Renson after he had delivered the money to them.

Aston Prior rose quite suddenly out of the plain; a fifteenth century church and an eighteenth century pub, a cluster of houses and a few shops. It would require inside knowledge to discover when the bank was worth robbing. But Skibby Thorne and his band had taken it for twenty-three thousand pounds. Paul drew up beside a barley field and announced that it was lunch time.

Steve was left to spread out the ground cloth and unpack the hamper while Paul disappeared into the pub. He was gone for twenty minutes, talking to the bored, talkative landlord over a sherry. He returned with a smug expression on his face and a bottle of superior vin rose.

"It was obviously our same three friends who called," he said, "and they drove off in the same direction, northwards. And they must have been tipped off."

Steve had served the cold chicken Veronique and rice salad on paper plates. It was delicious. Paul didn't even complain about the plastic containers the food had travelled in. He decided that he had misjudged Mrs. O'Hanrahan. The cheese and biscuits may have been left over from Christmas, but Mrs.

63

O'Hanrahan knew her chicken Veronique.

"How's the wine?" Paul asked.

"Perfect," said Steve. "I'm glad it's summer again."

They stayed in Aston Prior until half past two, basking in the sunshine and finishing the wine. Paul gave an edited account of his evening at the Love-Inn, dressing the girls in warmer clothes and making the stage show sound like the Television Toppers.

"You think Blane was waiting for Betty the other night, and that they stayed together at the motel?" said Steve.

"I think so. He must have been told to either incriminate her or get rid of her. People are disposable to Desmond Blane's boss."

"How could he incriminate her? The robberies have already taken place, and according to your theory the gang will be dispersing."

"Supposing she helps them to get the money out of the country? Blane could arrange to meet her in Ireland, and she could take the hundred thousand pounds over there for him."

"But surely," said Steve, "she wouldn't be so stupid!"

"In her present state she might do anything." Paul lit a cigarette, and then stared moodily at the book of matches inviting him to the Gateway Motel, Banbury. "In any case, Blane could probably fix it so that she carried the money over without even realising."

"You sound pessimistic, darling."

He nodded. "I wonder what they would do to her if they knew she had spoken to me."

Steve began clearing away the picnic litter. She was very tidy about it, putting all the paper plates and cups in a large bag to throw away and saving the plastic containers. That was when Paul saw the labels giving the price and the shop where they had been bought from.

"Come on," said Steve, "if we're going to reach Banham in

time for afternoon tea."

After Banham they drove home via Harkdale, but it was only a formality. Paul had confirmed his theory. The three banks were all branches of the same regional office, and indeed of the same national head office, which meant that only one inside man was required for the tip off.

"I'd say it was a man in the London office who told the gang when to pull the jobs," Paul said thoughtfully.

"Are you sure?"

"I think so, because the police turned up in Harkdale at the time of the robbery. A local man, even a man from Birmingham, could have discovered that the police car went through Harkdale at exactly the same time every Friday afternoon. Gavin Renson would have known, but he obviously took his orders from middle men."

"You mean this series of jobs was implemented suddenly."

"Yes. Something happened a month ago, so they had to move into action without the local groundwork which they should have done. That would also account for the way Betty was left in the air."

Steve took the empty hamper from the boot of the car and led Paul into the house. Mrs. O'Hanrahan had gone home, leaving them a cold chicken supper for the evening. Paul decided they would eat at the Gateway Motel, Banbury.

"Surely," said Steve, "the police ought to know who the bank robbers are. I mean the ones in the car, the police ought to know which gang they belonged to and who else has worked with them."

"They do." Paul went into the living room and sat in the armchair by the window. The sun had disappeared behind Snowshill leaving a chill reminder that summer was a few weeks off. "That was why I had breakfast with Charlie Vosper. They were members of the West London gang."

Paul took a pipe from the rack above the fireplace and filled it with tobacco. He smoked the pipe occasionally as a substitute for cutting out smoking.

"The West London gang," Charlie Vosper had said as he struck his third match, "Desmond Blane was their number two. I wondered what had happened to the rest of them."

"The rest?"

"It took me two years, but eventually I got them. I smashed up their operations and most of the gang went to gaol for several years. The boss was Joe Lancing. Did you know him?" Paul shook his head. "Fine bloke, I liked old Joe. He built the gang up from scratch just after the war. He was sentenced to fifteen years."

"So Blane got off?" Paul asked.

"Blane was out of the country, and some of the small fry slipped through, people like Skibby Thorne and Ray Norton. But it didn't matter much, because we'd broken up the gang. That was a year ago now."

Charlie Vosper talked nostalgically of his old friend Joe Lancing, of his rough childhood in Shepherd's Bush and the army surplus rackets, the black market business and street corner betting of his younger days. "He was a good lad. Won the D.S.O. in the war. He was the sort of villain you could talk to. But of course the world changed and Joe changed with it. Gambling became legal, the legitimate clubs made Joe's vice dens seem like pranks in a convent after lights out. He was earning thousands a week without breaking the law!"

They relaxed over the eggs and bacon. Paul enjoyed listening to Charlie Vosper when he was in this mood. It was probably because the Harkdale robbery wasn't his case: the bland grey haired inspector talked about his job and the opposition with affection.

"Of course there was protection and a few robberies. But in recent years Joe spent most of his energy with the investment of his loot. He bought property all over West London: office blocks and luxury flats and a couple of perfectly sound businesses. His boys were becoming fed up with the quiet life; they didn't think it was real money unless they had stolen it, and they resented the lawyers and the accountants who surrounded Joe. So Joe sometimes lent them out to the North London gang. That's where Skibby and his friends were when we got Joe, they were robbing a factory in North London. That's how they got off."

Charlie sipped his coffee sadly. "It was hardly worth locking Joe up."

"What did you get them for?"

"Fraud and a few tax infringements." In Charlie Vosper's book they weren't really crimes. "But it does go to show," he said triumphantly, "that we can catch the modern businessmen of the underworld. Did I ever tell you about the crash course I took in accountancy?"

"No," said Paul. He poured some more coffee. "Was it useful?"

"I'll say. I discovered how to reduce my income tax by a third. But the mistake you made on television last night was to assume that businessmen are intelligent. They only have to be good at their job, like anybody else." He chuckled to himself. "You wait until I retire in a couple of years. I'll go into business myself, and then you'll see what a copper is made of. I won't have Joe Lancing's capital investment to start me off, but I won't have his gang of dependents either."

Paul realised the man was being quite serious.

"Talking of dependents," said Paul, "there was a man called Arnold. About sixty, tall, with a northern accent. Was he one of the gang?"

Charlie Vosper thought not.

Charlie was not able to help much further, but he suggested a trip out to Coulsden open prison to see Joe. The West London gang no longer existed, and nobody had taken over from the old boss. "But Coulsden is on your way back to Broadway," said Charlie, "you've nothing to lose except half an hour of your time." The new brain behind the robberies was a stranger, probably a newcomer to crime. Charlie Vosper had admitted that such people were more difficult to identify than the usual villains who were merely difficult to arrest. But that was as far as he would go with Paul's thesis about change in the structure of crime.

Charlie Vosper had made the open prison sound like a Butlin's holiday camp, and the layout was similar. The main hall had a barred door which the Chief Warder unlocked from the familiar bundle of keys on his belt. The cream and green colour scheme and the flagstone floors, the range of furniture and the grey crumpled uniforms were much the same. It was open plan rather than unconfined.

"I'm Warder Druce," said the officer. "Inspector Vosper rang that you were coming." The door clanged ominously shut behind them. "Come through to the visitors' room."

Paul followed him down the corridor and round the three sides of a square upon which the administration block was built. He peered curiously into the rooms off, such as the recreation room, the television room, the gymnasium and a hall with a curtained stage. Just like a holiday camp. The prisoners whom they passed spoke with a slightly false cheerfulness and Druce bullied them into more vigorous effort.

"This seems a happy enough place," Paul said politely.

"Oh yes. A happy prison is an efficient prison." He led the way into a waiting room, with half a dozen chairs round a small central table. It was the room in which visitors were received and entertained. "Of course most of the prisoners are out at work now. They work out on the farms, and some go in to Coulsdon town to work in the factories. The ones you've seen on the premises are the new boys."

"Is Joe Lancing regarded as a new boy?"

"Oh yes, he only came four months ago." Druce chuckled indulgently. "But he nearly runs the place already. He soon found his way about."

Joe Lancing didn't look like a millionaire. He was about five feet six inches tall, and he had overgrown grey hair and bushy sideboards – the mark of a prisoner big enough to make his own rules. The red face of the heavy drinker explained the sagging figure: he should have had an overhanging stomach, but since he had been inside his girth had slumped. He was a scruffy, comfortable and amiable man.

"How's my old friend Vosper?" he asked gruffly. "Does he still keep my photograph above his bed, like Montgomery did with Rommel's photograph?" He shook hands, a large firm handshake that inspired confidence. "Sit down, make yourself comfortable."

Paul sat in an uncomfortable chair. He offered Joe a cigarette, but Joe insisted they smoke his.

"We have all your novels in the prison library," said Joe. "They aren't bad, except that all your villains are pretty unpleasant characters, and that isn't lifelike. I must introduce you to some of my friends. You'll like them."

"I'd like that," said Paul. "Actually it was one of your friends whom I wanted to ask you about. Desmond Blane—"

"Why don't you come and give a talk to our Literary Circle? They're a keen group of lads, some of them write thrillers and several are engaged on their autobiographies. I'll make that my price for any help I can give you."

Paul laughed and heard himself saying that of course he would be delighted to talk to the Literary Circle.

"That's agreed then. Now what were you saying about Des?"

"I wondered whether he was running your old outfit."

"Des?" Joe laughed appreciatively. "Des couldn't run his

69

own life. He's an old fashioned heavyweight who beats up the people you point him at."

"Somebody," Paul said carefully, "has been pointing him in the direction of three banks."

Joe stared in disbelief. "Why do you say that?"

"Because two of your men were killed getting away, Skibby Thorne and Larry Phillips, and another is critically injured in hospital. It seems as if Desmond Blane was their supervisor."

"Who's injured?" Joe asked.

"Ray Norton. I gather they were your goon squad."

Joe had risen to his feet and his face was flushed with ineffectual rage. "The silly buggers! I left them perfectly well provided for! Who put them up to it?"

"That's why I'm here," Paul murmured.

"Bloody cowboys," Joe said as he sat down again. "You can't let men like that out of your sight before they're up to some mischief." He shook his head with patriarchal resignation. "I can't help you, Mr. Temple. You would know more about their antics than I would. I only hear whispers in here, and I haven't heard any whispers about my boys robbing banks. They must have met somebody since I was sent down, fallen under a bad influence." He noticed the trace of a smile cross Warder Druce's face and snapped angrily, "No man was ever killed working for me, Mr. Druce."

The smile vanished.

"What," he asked Paul, "were your ideas?"

Paul explained as tactfully as he could that he thought there was a new number one on the London scene. "Obviously I wouldn't ask you to help me catch him, Mr. Lancing, that wouldn't be appropriate. But I thought you might tell me a few things about your old organisation."

Joe was silent for several moments, and then he murmured, "Well?"

"Desmond Blane ran your goon squad, didn't he? I wondered

whether he had a protection racket going, against the London clubs?"

"After a fashion," said Joe, "but there was nothing systematic about it. I allowed him to work the clubs just to keep the boys occupied."

"There's a club called the Love-Inn. Was that on his list?"

"No." The exiled boss shook his head and smiled. "I remember the Love-Inn, it's owned by an American. He told Des to do his worst. I think he was drunk at the time."

"What was Desmond Blane's worst?"

"The last I heard he was going out with one of the dancers there. Des was always easily diverted."

Paul described the man called Arnold, but he received no further information. Paul knew, of course, that Joe would avoid giving him any direct answers; Joe had other means than the law to keep order. But Paul thought he would be able to read the conversation behind the words. Joe Lancing did not know a man called Arnold. He had not heard of a new number one.

Which implied somebody who called in a few gangsters as required, rather than an empire builder of the old school. Joe had enjoyed his power, whereas the new man was out for the money.

Paul left the sprawling barracks of a prison feeling sad for the old man. There was a feeling of waste; he reminded Paul of a tiger in a zoo or Napoleon on St. Helena; it was a waste of his talent to be running a comfortable open gaol.

"How do you envisage the super-brain behind this crime?"

It was nine o'clock on the B 4035 to Banbury and Paul had been silent for the past half hour. Steve was driving the car. She pursed her lips unhelpfully.

"Do you envisage him as a kid from the Salford backstreets who cheated at the eleven plus and went to grammar school? A tough little kid who never got caught, passed his five G.C.E.s and then studied to be an accountant at evening classes? I expect we'll find he's about twenty-six and came into the scene as a financial adviser."

"Name of Jonathan Wild," Steve laughed.

They swung through the large illuminated entrance of the Gateway Motel, past the long bungalow shaped building and into the car park.

CHAPTER 7

THE Gateway Motel had been open for about six months. The owner was a sprightly little Scotsman called Angus Lomax. He had made his money by following the principle that what happens in America happens five years later in England, but the principle hadn't operated for motels. He came into the restaurant and looked at the sparse crowd with some apprehension.

Paul saw him ask the young manageress whom the Rolls outside belonged to. She nodded towards their table in the corner and added something which Paul couldn't read from her lip movements. Mr. Lomax came hurrying across to them.

The menu had a tendency towards the barbecue, with hot dogs and hamburgers featuring prominently, words like french fries and apple pie, but the waitress had looked relieved when Paul had ordered a rare steak with mashed potatoes. It was all a façade. When Steve had put on the juke box everybody had looked up in astonishment, including Paul.

"I only do it to keep you young," she explained to Paul. But she knew the records had been out of the hit parade since the motel opened.

There was one advantage to the place. If it were a meeting place for bank robbers Angus Lomax wouldn't be able to claim that he hadn't noticed them.

"Good evening, Mr. Temple. My daughter tells me you'd like a word."

Paul shook hands with him and invited him to sit down. He

could hardly say he was busy. "This is Steve, my wife." The man sat down.

"You have a very pleasant motel, Mr. Lomax," said Steve. "And a good chef. I'm surprised you aren't crowded tonight."

Those were the words to start Lomax talking. He relaxed into a long description of his troubles.

"Why don't you call this a hotel with ample parking accommodation?" Paul asked. "Then at least people would come for the food."

He shrugged. "We wouldn't attract the American visitors."

"I don't see any American visitors."

"It's a slack period," Lomax confessed unhappily. "But you didn't ask me across to hear about my problems. How can I help you, Mr. Temple?"

"I'm trying to trace the movements of a friend of mine," said Paul. "I think she stayed here the night before last."

"What's the name of your friend?"

Paul described Betty Stanway and explained that he thought the girl was probably in trouble. He could see from the way Angus Lomax was reacting that he was sympathetic, but he was no help.

"I'm absolutely sure she didn't stay here on Friday night." He smiled wryly. "I'm positive, because there wasn't a single member of the fair sex staying in the house on Friday. There were only three men."

Paul believed him. "Thank you, Mr. Lomax," he said quietly.

The man shook hands and went away with apologies for not being more help, hoping to see him at the Gateway again. Paul nodded and picked up another book of matches to remind himself.

"You're disappointed," Steve murmured.

He nodded. "I thought we had a lead."

"So what happens now?"

Paul put the matches in his pocket. "Let's go home." He signalled to the waitress and paid the bill.

They were in the hall when Steve remembered her handbag. She laughed and went back to fetch it. Paul waited, deep in thought. He watched his wife walk across the restaurant with the black patent leather handbag. He had an idea.

"Is Mr. Lomax still in the building?" he asked the young manageress.

"I believe so." She knocked on one of the doors off the hall and poked her head into the office. "Hello, Daddy. Will you have another word with Mr. Temple?"

Steve came into the hall in time to be left behind. "I shan't be a minute, darling. I'll see you in the car." She looked surprised, but she went out to the car park.

Paul explained to Angus Lomax that he had probably been too specific in his enquiry. Maybe Betty Stanway hadn't spent the night there – motels weren't only for sleeping, were they? He described Desmond Blane, and for good measure he mentioned the sixty year old northerner called Arnold. This time he was lucky.

"I know Arnold Cookson," said Lomax. "He's been here for lunch half a dozen times in the past six months. There is usually a man of about thirty, a big smartly dressed man, he could be Desmond what's-his-name. But he isn't local. Anyway, what is this? What are they supposed to have done? Shipped unsuspecting Midlands girls to London?"

While Paul explained that a series of bank robberies had taken place and, as the formula had it, the police wanted to interview these men in connection with their enquiries, Angus Lomax swung round to look out of the window. He was looking at the row of sleeping cabins.

"The big one," said Paul, "the one we're assuming to have been Desmond Blane. Did he ever come here with anyone else apart from Cookson?"

"Only once. And I'm pretty hopeless with descriptions of people."

It was a delicate situation, and Paul could sympathise with the man; he had invested a lot of money and most of his life in this motel; and already, without any scandal attaching to the place, it was failing. Mr. Lomax had his own problems with the banks.

"In your experience, Mr. Temple, does a reputation for running the ideal meeting ground for bank robbers lead to increased business or ruin?"

Paul laughed. "All publicity is good publicity. Where do I find Arnold Cookson?"

"I don't know," said Lomax. "He's disappeared. Rumour has it he went broke and he's hiding from his creditors, but I don't believe it. He was a very rich man." Lomax spoke with the instinctive bitterness of a man who has very little.

"When did he disappear?" asked Paul.

"About three weeks ago, but people claim to have seen him around since then. He hasn't gone far." Lomax looked suddenly worried. "Perhaps I shouldn't be telling you all this. I wouldn't want to shop a man for robbing a bank."

"Don't worry about that," said Paul. "He isn't Robin Hood. A number of people have died because of those bank robberies."

Paul decided that Steve deserved a new handbag. Crocodile, of course, that was what she had hinted she needed for her birthday. Paul decided to buy her a crocodile un-birthday present as soon as the case was over.

"Why are you looking so pleased with yourself?" Steve asked as he climbed into the car.

"I've decided to buy you a new handbag."

Paul even made the cocoa when they got back to the cottage. He knew how she hated her plans for a peaceful holiday to go chaotically adrift. But she was bearing up remarkably well. Tonight indeed she had been inadvertently very helpful. When

Paul arrived with the cocoa she was already in bed.

"Are you fed up?" he asked her.

"I've been married to you for a long time," she said with a laugh.

There was a screeching sound from the depths of the garden, a barn owl or perhaps a frightened badger. Paul listened as he sipped his cocoa. He wondered what noises a badger makes.

"Come to bed," Steve murmured.

"Do you think my villains are dislikeable?" he asked her.

"Darling, it's nearly one o'clock."

He had decided to lecture the open prisoners on Criminals and the Myth of the Outsider. It sounded suitably academic and yet trendy, the kind of thing the colour supplements might like. Perhaps he would repeat it to those Townswomen who kept pestering him to address their Guild. In his experience most criminals tended to be unintelligent and conformist, which was a shame because it made them less interesting than they sounded. They were hostile to authority , of course—

"Steve!"

She had thrown a pillow at him.

"I nearly spilled my cocoa."

She sat up in bed and tossed her hair temperamentally. "This is a new and very sexy nightdress, and you haven't even noticed it! I've been lying demurely in bed for fifteen minutes and you haven't even looked at me! I'm going to sleep!" She lay down again and simultaneously turned off the light. "And if you don't stop laughing I'll throw the *other* pillow at you."

Paul climbed happily into bed beside her.

CHAPTER 8

STEVE was not accustomed to spending long periods in the country alone; she was accustomed to the irritation of Paul being constantly about as she tried to finish a design. The clatter of his typewriter overhead, the pause before he came downstairs in search of a particular word or a reference or a cup of coffee, and then at the sight of Mrs. O'Hanrahan fleeing back to continue typing: that was the pattern of life in Broadway. She wasn't used to silence.

Paul had gone off to see Inspector Manley. He had an idea that Arnold Cookson would be known to the local police since he had local connections. Steve wondered whether to pass the morning in search of Cookson, just to show that she could have been a detective if she had chosen a career instead of a husband. The man from the garage in the village had returned her Hillman Imp that morning. It had been in for a new dynamo since Christmas and the mechanic had been sarcastic about people who forgot where they left their cars. Steve wanted to try the car out.

"I could see he was worried, dear, as soon as he came to the door and asked for Mr. Temple. I knew there was something wrong—"

It was the ninth time of telling and each time the story acquired several additional details, most of which showed an increase in Mrs. O'Hanrahan's intuitive wisdom and natural sympathy.

"I came back when he'd gone to tell the man from the public

opinion poll—"

"Who?" Steve asked with sudden attention.

"The man from the public opinion. He wanted to know how we voted and what we thought of the newspapers."

"What did you tell him?"

"I said Paul always took *The Times* to do the crossword—"

"No, no, Mrs. O'Hanrahan, what did you tell him about Gavin Renson?"

"Nothing." She smiled benignly at Steve's thick headedness. "He wasn't here, was he? He'd gone."

"I don't know, Mrs. O'Hanrahan, you've never mentioned this visitor before."

"Well, he wasn't important. He went away." Mrs. O'Hanrahan ran carelessly into the garden calling at Jackson to leave her best gladioli alone! Steve watched in amusement. She was beginning to understand why Paul found the woman difficult.

"I'm going out for a walk," Steve announced when Mrs. O'Hanrahan returned with the dog. "I need a breath of fresh air." She patted the dog and asked him whether he wanted to come as well. It appeared that he did.

Steve had bought him a lead, but whenever she put it on him he sat on his hind legs and sulked. Once more she went through the established ritual of putting on the lead, dragging Jackson into the drive and then releasing him. Mrs. O'Hanrahan said something about not teaching old dogs new tricks.

"I think we'll go into Banbury," said Steve.

"You'll need a heavier pair of shoes than those little slingbacks," Mrs. O'Hanrahan declared. "It's a long walk."

"We'll go by car."

Jackson sat in the back seat and barked at all the passing motorists as if he were accustomed to the English traffic. On quieter stretches of the road across to Banbury he sniffed the back of Steve's neck, and then just as they reached the town he lay down and went to sleep. Steve pulled up outside the public library.

In the hallowed silence which was the nearest local government aspired to godliness, Steve tried the obvious reference books. The telephone directory, the local chamber of commerce directory and asking the library assistant whether Cookson was in the borrowers' register.

"I'm sorry," the librarian said primly, "we can't give you information like that. After all, we don't know who you are."

"Mrs. Temple," said Steve. "Do you want to see my driving licence?"

He stuck to his rectitude. "I meant that you might be a debt collector or his ex-wife, something like that."

"I'm a detective and I suspect Mr. Cookson of being a bank robber."

"Ha ha," he brayed in the cathedral hush, "Mr. Cookson wouldn't need to rob a bank. His bank manager calls him sir."

"Do you know him?"

"Of course. He owns the estate agents office round the corner."

The estate agents round the corner was called Kimber & Sons. When Steve climbed out of the car she realised that Jackson had woken up and was more than usually excited. He jumped across the seat onto the pavement and ran barking to the office door. Steve followed him.

"Oh gawd, look who it is!" said the receptionist.

Steve was taken aback. "I beg your pardon?"

But the chemically blonde receptionist had scarcely noticed Steve. "Get out, Jackson, before I call the vivisectionists!" The dog had jumped up at her in recognition. They were clearly old enemies. "If you ladder my stockings—"

"Down, Jackson," Steve said firmly.

"Now look at my stockings!" snapped the girl. She glared at Steve, but her voice was precisely correct. "I'm sorry, can I help you?"

"I wanted to see Mr. Cookson."

"He isn't here. Do you know this dog?"

"Yes," said Steve hanging on to his collar, "I'm looking after him."

"You aren't looking after him very well." She glanced quickly at Steve to see whether it was safe to continue the attack, and obviously she decided it was not. "Where's Gavin then?"

"He's dead."

"Gavin?" Her eyes strayed back to the dog in superstitious fear. "What happened?" She backed away from the dog as if he were tainted with death. "There was nothing wrong with Gavin."

"He was murdered," Steve said gently. "How did you come to know him?"

"He worked here."

"I'm sorry."

"Who murdered him?"

"I don't know. The police are still working on it."

The girl talked about Gavin's charm and how he used to drive the customers out to look at properties for sale. It gave her time to regain her composure. She explained that he had joined the firm soon after Mr. Cookson had arrived from Liverpool and bought himself a partnership. She began repainting her fingernails and explained that Gavin had been sacked a month ago for taking the dog everywhere.

"It didn't look good with the customers, you see."

"Was business falling off?" Steve asked.

"You could say that," she agreed. "This is a bad time for selling property." She told Steve about the tragic fate of several speculative builders in that part of the country and the sad lull in the lives of the big developers. "Mr. Kimber would have gone bankrupt if it hadn't been for Mr. Cookson turning up like that. We were lucky. Mr. Cookson has imagination and flair." The girl paused suspiciously. "Did you say you wanted to see Mr.

Cookson? "

"Yes."

"We don't know where he is." She resumed her professional manner. "Can somebody else help?"

"I don't think so. He's a personal friend of mine; I live over in Broadway. Last time he came to dinner I lent him my copy of the Chamber of Commerce directory, and I wanted it back. It's a small blue book—"

"I think I've seen it," the receptionist said helpfully.

"Do you think perhaps we could—?"

"Why not?"

Steve followed her into Arnold Cookson's empty office. She deliberately shut Jackson out, and he howled loudly while the girl flipped through the papers on the desk.

"Shall I look?" asked Steve, "if you could keep Jackson happy. I mean, I know what the directory is like."

The telephone was ringing as well. The girl smiled gratefully and left Steve alone in the office.

Five minutes later Steve went back to the girl and retrieved Jackson. She hadn't found a blue directory, thank goodness, but she had picked up half a dozen possible ideas. She thanked the receptionist.

"Oh, by the way," Steve said by the door, "what is so important about Red Trees Farm?"

"Nothing now. Mr. Cookson was going to build a housing estate, but it all fell through. It's used as a caravan site, and Mr. Cookson sold it to a customer in London."

Steve drove back to Broadway deep in thought. The most baffling thing was why Cookson had bought himself an estate agent's business, unless he was genuinely an estate agent, in which case why was he robbing banks? She assumed he was not the super-brain because of the way Desmond Blane had referred to him on the telephone. And why had he disappeared? He must have left quite a sum of money tied up in Kimber &

Sons.

The very quick examination of Cookson's desk had indicated that he had worked busily for the good of the firm. But it was possible that the bank robbers were hiding out in a property that had passed through his hands. Steve tested the car's newly repaired condition as she sped across the hills, turned into Buckle Street and swooped eventually down to the village.

She nearly crashed as she reached Random Cottage. Paul was emerging from the drive in the Rolls and he was wearing that don't-stop-me-I'm-in-a-hurry expression. Steve pressed the horn in exasperation and Jackson began barking again.

"Where are you going?" Steve called.

"I came back to see whether you were bored," he said. "The police are probably off to arrest Blane and Cookson. I didn't want to disappear for hours without letting you know."

Steve bent over and kissed him through the car window. "Have you ever heard of Red Trees Farm?" she asked casually.

"Yes. Funnily enough that's where we're off to. Bye bye."

She watched the Rolls disappear along the road, did not respond to Paul's cheery wave of farewell, and then turned back to the Hillman and kicked the rear nearside tyre.

CHAPTER 9

"PAUL TEMPLE has been asking for me in town," said Arnold Cookson.

"It doesn't matter. We'll be gone by the time he traces you to this godforsaken place."

"Doesn't matter? The police will be on to me!"

Desmond Blane chuckled to himself. Everywhere you go, for the rest of your life, you'll be on the run. At any time of the day or night, whenever there's a knock at the door or a hand falls on your shoulder, it could be the last arrest. You'll never be able to relax, or allowed to forget. A hunted man with a false identity. That was how the dialogue went, from one of those old Humphrey Bogart films. And all it meant was that Arnold would spend the rest of his life like he'd spent the first sixty years.

"They know your name as well," said Arnold.

"That bastard Renson must have talked."

"Perhaps you were right after all," muttered Arnold. "Perhaps you did have to kill him."

"Don't start on that again!"

They were getting on each other's nerves. Desmond had always been a Londoner. He found the old man's accent jarring, and he certainly didn't like being cooped up with him. The sight of sheep grazing out of the caravan windows first thing in the mornings was spoiling his taste for mutton. The country was all right for chawbacons like Arnold, but if Desmond never saw another farm he would die happy.

"Are you going to kill Temple?" asked Arnold.

"Not unless it becomes necessary."

Arnold Cookson snorted. "You mean not unless you're told to. I'm glad this is nearly over. I've never worked for a boss like ours before."

"It isn't the boss's fault that Renson cracked." Desmond shuffled the cards and began another game of patience with himself. "Renson was your contact, you said you knew him like your own son."

"I don't know why he went to see Paul Temple."

I know, thought Desmond Blane. He thought we were double crossing him. He had arrived the morning after the robbery full of boyish glee, the money in his bag and the dog barking behind him. And then he had learnt that the heat was on. The men who had pulled the job smashed up in the car, a policeman dead and a bank clerk injured. There wasn't much to be gleeful about.

"We're pulling out on Monday evening," Blane had said. "It's been a nice ride, but it's over." He had taken the bag from Gavin Renson and tossed it under the bunk.

"Where will you be going?"

Cookson had said abroad.

"So what about my cut? We've lifted more than a hundred thousand quid and so far I haven't seen—"

"We'll settle up, don't worry."

But Renson had eaten his breakfast in gloomy dissatisfaction. "I won't know where to find you. I don't even know who we've been working for." He kept tossing pieces of bacon on to the caravan floor for the dog, which had irritated Desmond Blane. "Who have we been working for?"

"You don't need to know."

"A fellow in the paper this morning calls him a super-brain of crime, a new kind of businessman." Renson had pointed to the newspaper article. "Paul Temple, you see? He lives over there, across the hills. I've read some of his books."

"Okay, so you can read. You know the arrangement—"

"I know. You owe me ten thousand pounds. Don't forget that in your panic to escape, or you'll read all about these robberies in Mr. Temple's next newspaper article."

That was his death sentence.

He realised he had said too much, Desmond Blane could see the fear in the kid's eyes, and he left without drinking his coffee.

"He'll be all right," Arnold Cookson had said nervously as they watched the lorry with its authentic load of gravel disappear along the track. "I can't see Gavin shopping us."

"Neither can I." Desmond Blane could imagine vividly what the prospect of death or not receiving his cut could do to a young man like Renson. "I won't let him."

It preoccupied him for the rest of the morning, and at lunch time he decided to telephone London. There was a phone box about a mile down the lane which was their link with the world.

Blane drove a decently anonymous black Triumph 1300; it wasn't a getaway car or a status symbol. He had built up a resentment against driving it along the track to the caravan farm, but he drove it this time to the public call box.

He dialled a London telephone number, and while he was waiting to be put through he looked up Paul Temple in the local directory. Random Cottage, it was entered, Broadway. No number or street.

"Okay, Des," the voice on the other end instructed, "take whatever action you find is necessary. Keep an eye on Paul Temple's home." They discussed the sudden changes in schedule. "By the way, there's a slight problem this end as well. I think you're the best person to help —"

He drove over the hills to Broadway. It was a crowded village in the bowl of a valley. The central street was very wide and sloped up through a clutter of houses and shops and gardens, but Blane could not see any sign indicating Random Cottage. Eventually he went into the Lygon Arms and asked the girl behind the reception desk.

"It's up Fish Hill," she said. "You'll see a turning on the right as you leave the village."

Blane stayed for a large whisky and watched the village life passing by. There were a couple of farmers in the lounge talking barley; they made him yearn for the racing chat of his own pub in the Brompton Road. But when he found himself wondering whether he would ever see it again he realised he was going soft. He was here to do a job.

Random Cottage was actually a house, he found. He strode up to the front door and hammered on the knocker. Full frontal assault. He announced that he was engaged in market research, asking questions about the newspapers people read, Mrs. Temple.

"I'm Mrs. O'Hanrahan," the woman declared with a shriek of laughter. "I live down the road by the post office."

"You'll do, if Mrs. Temple isn't in." She was a formidable woman, but she seemed pleased to have company. "Can we go inside and talk?"

She took Desmond Blane through to the kitchen and told him about her reading habits, about the late Paddy O'Hanrahan, may he rest in peace, about her life, and Mr. Temple and his little foibles.

"He reads newspapers," she announced impressively. "Mr. Temple always does the crossword, but he cheats. He looks up the quotations in a dictionary."

"I seem to remember that he writes for one of the papers."

"He's very clever." She nodded and hitched up her bra strap. "He's got a terribly pretty wife."

"A series of articles on the gang scene—"

"She's a designer."

"Really? I expect there have been a lot of reactions to the articles. People coming to the house and so on?"

"Terribly natural, she is, talks to you just like an ordinary person like you or me."

"Thank you," he sighed.

To his relief there was a knock at the door and Mrs. O'Hanrahan bustled out to answer it. Desmond Blane wondered how he could keep her to the point. She was so talkative that it was impossible to get information from her. He heard the voice at the front door asking for Paul Temple.

"He won't be here until tomorrow," she was saying.

The man at the door was Gavin Renson! He could hear the kid saying it didn't matter, he only wanted to discuss a series of newspaper articles . . .

Desmond Blane left the kitchen by the side door. He saw the lorry in the lane, and a few moments later Renson went down the path, climbed into the driver's cabin and left. Blane hurried after him.

He caught up with Renson just past the Fish Inn.

"I don't know why he went to see Paul Temple."

The caravan was getting on Desmond's nerves. The smell of calor gas, the buckets of water that had to be fetched from a communal tap, and the chemical toilets on the other side of the field. They didn't seem to worry Arnold Cookson. Thirty-seven times yesterday Arnold had said, "Nature calls!" and thirty-seven times he had trotted happily across to the bog. There was something wrong with his tubes! It worried Desmond Blane.

"I hope to God we can trust your girlfriend," said Arnold.

"What do you mean, trust her? We don't need to trust her, because she won't know what she's carrying."

"If there's any doubt about her—"

"There isn't. We'll be in Dublin tomorrow."

"What time is she supposed to be ringing?"

"Twelve o'clock, on the dot." Blane glanced at his watch. "Yes, I'd better get down to the call box." He picked up the jacket from his bunk, swung it over his shoulder, and left the caravan. It was five to twelve so he took the car.

The telephone box was empty. Desmond reversed the car and sat in it while he waited for the call. He waited for five and a half minutes. His irritation began to mount as the hands of the car clock moved away from the hour. She was a silly bitch. Just a silly little bitch who had thought he was rich. He remembered how impressed she had been with the penthouse. And she always drank so much that she fell asleep in the middle of making love. Three times that had happened! But she could be trusted. The silly bitch was in love with him.

Eventually he got out of the car and went into the telephone kiosk. He picked up the receiver to dial and then paused. The line was dead. "Sod," he breathed. He stayed in the kiosk and pretended to be speaking to someone as two police cars raced by.

Desmond Blane gave them two minutes and then followed carefully back to the caravan site. He saw the police cars in the field while a uniformed policeman stood at the gate. Desmond accelerated and drove straight past. He narrowly missed a Rolls that was coming in from the opposite direction. They hooted at each other and passed by.

Paul Temple pulled up at the Red Trees Caravan Site and recovered his nerve. He didn't like people who drove cars straight at him. The police were busily making their arrests, they didn't appear to need any help from him. But Paul wandered across to have a look at the villains.

"There's only one," Inspector Manley said gruffly. "This is Arnold Cookson."

"Good morning," said Paul. He was about sixty, quite tall, with a northern accent. "Where's Desmond Blane?"

"Who?" Cookson continued to assert that he was a simple holidaymaker. "Why don't you try the caravan next door? There must be some mistake."

After warning Cookson the Inspector said "I'm arresting you for murder, robbery with violence, conspiring—"

"I'm not saying another word!"

A policeman had been systematically searching the caravan. He pulled a suitcase from underneath one of the bunks and asked Arnold Cookson for the key.

"I don't have a key. That isn't my suitcase."

He watched tensely while the policeman prised the case open with a small penknife. The case was empty.

"The money!" Cookson gasped. "Where's the money?"

Inspector Manley smiled. "It looks as if you've been double-crossed, Arnold. You'd better tell me who your friends are."

"There was more than a hundred grand in that case!"

"So where is it? Come along, Arnold, don't be loyal. Who runs this litde outfit of yours?"

Cookson was white faced and his mouth trembled as he spoke. "I don't know. Desmond Blane was the only one I knew."

It appeared to be true that Cookson's only known superior was Blane, for the police were unable to shift him from this in two hours of close and detailed questioning. Paul sat on the bunk at the end of the caravan and watched the dogged Inspector Manley tie the man up in conclusive detail.

"You might as well tell us everything," the inspector said, "because we know most of it, including that nice little pose of being a respectable estate agent."

"I'm a genuine estate agent," Cookson insisted. "There's a certificate on the wall of my office with the charter—"

"I know, I know, you qualified nineteen years ago in Liverpool. We've had your records sent through to us. Nineteen years ago you were obviously determined to make a new start. But it didn't last long, did it? You were soon back inside."

"I meant to go straight this time," said Cookson.

Inspector Manley chuckled. "Is that what you call it? You were released from Parkhurst six months ago, you collected the loot that had been waiting for you and came out here to make another new start. But this didn't last long either, did it? What happened?

Arnold Cookson was smoking cigarette after cigarette while he talked of how badly the slump in housing had hit the estate agent business. He knew that his tobacco ration would be limited for the next few years.

"I'd only recently bought myself a partnership in Kimber & Son. I put every penny I had into the business, and then the bloody government had to produce another credit squeeze. The mortgage position is impossible—"

"So what happened?" Manley interrupted.

Cookson had been enjoying a few gins in the Black Bear one evening when Desmond Blane had approached him. It had seemed like a casual meeting, yet Blane knew all there was to know about him. He had known about the prison record, and more important he had known how desperate were his present business arrangements.

"Blane had a series of bank jobs lined up, and they were to happen in quick succession. That would be the end of it, a quick swoop and I would be paid sixty thousand pounds." He smiled a nervous, tobacco stained smile. "I couldn't refuse, could I?"

"What was your part in the raids?" asked Manley.

"I planned them, of course. I worked out the strategy. They call me Field Marshal Cookson."

Paul wondered whether Cookson could be the super-brain, but it was most unlikely. There was more to robbing banks than robbing banks. And Cookson was a graduate of the early borstals, he had spent all his life in and out of prison. He would not suddenly become a man who gave orders.

"I had to draw up the plans for the raids and submit them through Desmond Blane for approval. I was told which bank and what day the raid would be on, and I had to work out what was necessary to pull it off."

"Were the plans approved?" Paul intervened.

"The boss made a few modifications." He thought for a moment and then added reluctantly, "They were sound modifications too."

"Who was the boss?"

But Cookson didn't know. He didn't even know much about the bank raiders who actually did the job. Paul had to admire the way the super-brain had acquired his men and then kept them apart. Arnold Cookson and his assistant Gavin Renson had put in the local fieldwork together for several months, and that was almost the end of their work. Renson had to pick up the money and bring it to the caravan. Arnold had to stay with Blane to keep an eye on the schedules.

"Did it all go according to schedule?" asked Manley.

"More or less, until Harkdale. The trouble was that it was suddenly put ahead by a month, so we had to rush things. I didn't know about the Harkdale job until a month ago. If we had kept to the original timetable we wouldn't have met that patrol car."

"And perhaps," said Manley, "the money would still be here in the suitcase."

"Perhaps." Arnold Cookson glowered at the empty case. "That bloody girlfriend of Blane's must have taken it back to London. I knew there was something going on. She slept here the night before last."

"That sounds cosy."

"Cosy? They were bouncing around on that bunk like rabbits until four o'clock in the morning. The caravan lurched three feet further into the field." He sighed. "I suppose she's taking the money to safety. We were supposed to be going to Ireland for the shareout, but that's off now. I'll never see Ireland again. Or my share of the money."

"What was this girl's name?" Manley asked.

"Betty Stanway."

"Ah." He looked complacently at Paul. "You were right, Temple."

"Of course."

Arnold Cookson rose to his feet. "I've smoked all my cigarettes. We might as well be going." He looked around the caravan for the last time, glanced at the cows on the far side of the field, and walked out to meet his sentence. He accepted defeat with dignity.

Paul watched the police car drive away with its prisoner, waved in acknowledgement to the two constables who had remained to make routine enquiries on the site, and then he headed for London.

"Who was that?" P.C. Newby asked. "The Chief Constable?"

"Paul Temple," said Brooks. "He talks about crime on television."

Newby hammered on another caravan door. "Sounds like a better life than being a policeman."

He wondered why people should take their holidays in May. Or why they should take them in a field near Banbury. But it seemed that very few people did. They were mostly owned by the high fliers of Birmingham who came out for the weekends. They found three people in residence, and they were the three wise monkeys.

"No, I never saw anybody go near that caravan. What was supposed to be going on?"

"No, I never heard a thing. I didn't know there had been a bank robbery."

"I can't talk to you now, I've got a hangover and my

husband's at work."

The one with a hangover was a young blonde and Newby watched his colleague disappear into her caravan with cheerful assurances that he knew an old gypsy cure.

It would serve P.C. Brooks right if he did get chucked out of the force, he thought. When that report on how he had smashed up another police car reached the divisional superintendent it ought to be his lot. Which would be a relief. Brooks was already getting on his nerves, and they had only been driving together for two days.

Bob Newby plodded slowly up the hill to the farmhouse. Perhaps after all it was lucky that he was alone. He might stumble on something important, and as this was the biggest case that had ever come his way he would like to be the lone hero. It would make sure of that promotion.

But there was only an old man in the house, and he didn't know anything either. He looked after the bookings for the caravan site, supplied them with milk and newspapers, and made sure the council took away the refuse.

Bob Newby plodded down the hill again. He hated farms. He found P.C. Brooks leaning over a fence and stroking a cow in the next field. Not a care in the world.

"Any luck?" Newby asked him.

"Not this time, but I'll be back. She's staying here all through the summer."

"That wasn't what I meant."

CHAPTER 10

DESMOND BLANE looked ruffled, there was a glint in his eyes from a frightening light and his hair needed combing. All men look like dangerous criminals in their C.R.O. photographs, but Desmond Blane looked like some other criminal. They would never catch him by issuing that to the newspapers, Paul decided. Underneath the photograph was a caption which referred ironically to Blane as "the darkly good-looking London company director, whom the police wish to interview in connection with the series of Midlands bank raids."

While Paul was reflecting on the poor quality of criminal records he realised that this was the man who had driven straight at him that morning. They had missed capturing him by thirty seconds, and by failing to circulate his photograph earlier. It was an impressive record: only one conviction, for armed robbery at the age of eighteen. Blane was not a petty crook.

"Inspector Vosper will see you now, Mr. Temple."

Paul went into his office. A cluttered, smoke filled den that looked onto a courtyard. Charlie Vosper was putting away an empty sandwich tin and trying to look as if he had been working.

"Just been setting the hounds onto Desmond Blane," he said as he waved to a chair. "You've seen the photograph? One of our mug shots. That'll find the bastard. Give us forty-eight hours and the case will be cleared up nicely."

Paul wondered whether they had forty-eight hours to

spare.

"Maybe not, but all we can do is ask around, circularise his old haunts and interview his known acquaintances. Otherwise we'll have to wait for him. We'll have him if he appears at one of the airports, don't worry."

"Have you put a man onto Betty Stanway?"

Inspector Vosper was evasive. "We're looking into that."

"What do you mean?"

"I mean we can't find the damned kid."

"But she's in danger—"

"We've notified the airport authorities in Dublin. What more can we do?"

"She won't go to Dublin now."

Vosper picked up the coffee cup from the top of his files and emptied the cold dregs with a grimace.

"This is marvellous," Paul said wearily. "We've cleared up all the small fry, and now the people in the centre of this case have all vanished. Do you know what's likely to happen? The organising mind behind all this is going to get away with it!"

Charlie Vosper nodded cheerfully. "Those provincial police forces do their best, Temple, and of course it's a point of pride with them not to call in the Yard—"

Police politics! Paul ducked the whole issue. "There are obviously two channels to the organising mind. The first channel, from the gang which carried out the robberies, is through Desmond Blane. But there is a second channel. From inside the banks, through the person who provided the inside information. It's my guess that person is in London—"

"I already thought of it," said Vosper. "The bank's head office is letting me have a list of all its staff, with a note on those who have access to information about large transfers of money."

"The inside man may have left the bank suddenly, about four weeks ago. I think that must have been the reason the robbers decided to move their schedule forward."

"I hadn't finished," Vosper said. "I asked for a special list of all employees who left within the last ten weeks."

"Good thinking, Charlie."

"I've been doing quite a bit of thinking during the lunch hour. I've decided you could be right." He puffed at his pipe encouragingly. "If we must have your whizz kids coming into crime, what better place for them to come from than the banks? They'll be trained in accountancy, grammar-school boys with a bit of further education. I think we might find that our inside man is a very interesting character. He would be meticulous, a good organisation man. I'm looking forward to meeting him."

Vosper reached for his hat and opened the door in one practised movement as he stood up. "Well, are you coming to pick up that list of names with me?"

The bank head office was in Leadenhall Street, and as a police car drove them along the Strand and Fleet Street and past St. Paul's there was time to reflect on Inspector Vosper's objectives. He was troubled, because he wanted someone to put on trial for the death of that policeman in Harkdale. It wasn't enough that the man who had shot P.C. Felton was also dead. Inspector Vosper believed in justice being seen to be done, and that troubled him. He didn't like his emotions to be involved in a case.

"They're holding his funeral tomorrow," said Charlie. "But I'm not going. I've seen too many funerals, I can imagine Harry Felton's wife, a nice country girl with a couple of happily unimaginative kids, and I know how angry it would make me feel. The trouble with being a copper is that getting shot at is all part of the job."

Paul knew what an effort it was for Charlie Vosper to put his quite complex feelings into words. "Crime is an emotional business," Paul said lamely. "There's a lot of suffering behind the baldly stated facts."

Vosper stared at the Mansion House as they passed. There was some kind of city reception on, and a sergeant directing the V.I.P. traffic saluted them. "I hope you're wrong about them using Betty Stanway to get the money out of the country. She'll be another casualty, especially if they've changed their plans and won't be using her."

Leadenhall Street appeared to be a street of bank head offices that shaded off into a street of shipping offices, and the police car drew up exactly where it became confusing. There was a stationery shop and a café on either side of the building which they went into. They asked for the area manager, because Charlie Vosper believed in avoiding directors and company spokesmen.

"Your name, sir?" asked the uniformed attendant.

"Inspector Vosper and Mr. Temple."

They stood and watched the staff on the ground floor watching them while the attendant made a series of muted telephone calls. Charlie Vosper looked, even in his smart grey civvy suit, like a policeman. Paul wondered what they thought he was. The bustling room was divided by partitions into about thirty sections, telephones rang in every corner and messengers carried papers from sections and customers and disappeared through doors. Paul turned his attention to the notice which offered five hundred pounds reward to any person giving information that would lead to a conviction for bank robberies.

"If you'll come this way, gentlemen. Mr. Joseph Jeffcote will see you." He showed them into the lift. "Mr. Joseph Jeffcote is one of the bank's directors."

Charlie Vosper grunted unhappily.

It was a massive office on the fifth floor, flanked with secretaries and other directors' offices. Oak panelling and solid banking respectability. Mr. Joseph Jeffcote wore a black jacket and pin striped trousers. A large man with a face flushed with capillary veins. He reminded Paul in some respects of Joe Lancing, but the voice was noticeably different.

"Sit down, gentlemen," he barked. "I've sent for the area manager, he won't be a moment. Delighted to meet you. Temple? Well, well, I saw you on television, and I tell you that as it's my bank's branches that have been robbed I don't agree with you that things should be made easier for the criminals." He laughed inappropriately. "I'd send them to gaol for thirty years."

"I think you must have misunderstood what I said," Paul murmured.

Mr. Joseph Jeffcote spoke with spasmodic and forceful bursts of words, like a man who has overcome a stammer. "Ah, Benson, come in. These are the lists, are they?" He took them and started to read them.

The area manager had turned to leave.

"If Mr. Benson could stay," Vosper said courteously. "He might be able to help."

"Benson?" He clearly thought it unlikely. "As you wish. Can you spare us a moment, Benson?"

He could.

"Inspector Vosper," Jeffcote said as he surveyed the lists, "I must be under a misapprehension. These lists concern our head office staff. Are you not investigating the robberies in our south-west-midlands area?"

Vosper shook his head. "The south-west-midlands area man is Inspector Manley. He's in charge of the case out there, but I'm helping him with the London end."

"And what might the London end be?"

"We think somebody in this building tipped off the bank robbers about times and the movements of money which the banks would be handling."

"It's unheard of."

Vosper smiled unpleasantly. "I often hear about things like

that. So could I see the lists? We think it quite probable that the inside man left these offices about a month ago. Perhaps he was transferred to a branch or even sacked."

Paul moved in closer to Vosper and peered over his shoulder. There had not been a great deal of staff movement. Adams, Jarvis, Miss Pinkerton, Sampson, Wilks. And three people had been transferred by way of their promotion. The Miss Pinkerton had left to be married.

"Sampson," Paul murmured. "Is this Tony Sampson?"

Mr. Joseph Jeffcote looked enquiringly at Benson.

"Mr. Anthony Sampson, yes, sir. He was in the accounts department, but we suggested he might find a position that would be more congenial. He wasn't quite the type."

Paul smiled. "What type is that?"

"Well, sound, you know, solid. Sampson wasn't my sort of chap at all. He always needed a haircut and his clothes were what I can only describe as sharp. We have to watch things like that, you know. Besides, he had a drink problem and apparently frequented rather dubious haunts in his spare time."

"We dispensed with his services?" asked Jeffcote.

"I used my own initiative, Mr. Joseph. There were some very strange rumours, and one of the girls claimed she saw him copying out the security van's delivery schedule. We couldn't have that kind of information spread around.

Charlie Vosper sounded slightly apoplectic. "She saw what?"

"Copying the delivery schedules into his notebook." He rinsed his hands nervously. 'Well, what would you have done?"

"Changed the delivery schedule?" suggested Vosper.

"Oh." The area manager began to perspire. "You don't think he—? I mean, do you suppose those bank robberies—? My goodness me!"

His address was in the staff records as Tite Street, Chelsea.

"Isn't that rather expensive?" asked Paul. The only other fellow he could think of who had lived in Tite Street had died penniless in France, but that had been in 1930.

"Very expensive. We paid Mr. Sampson £1750 per annum, but I'd put his standard of living at five thousand a year minimum. He was, I think you would agree, flashy. Drove about in a white Jaguar. I knew I was right to dismiss him."

Charlie Vosper was silent as they went down in the lift. He didn't speak until they were in the police car and heading towards Chelsea. Then the inspector spoke a few terse words about banks who just ask to be robbed and clerks who think it will never happen to them.

"By the way," he said nastily to Paul, "how come you knew of Tony Sampson? You didn't mention him to me."

"Oh, he just cropped up briefly the other day. There was no reason to attach any importance to him then."

Vosper coughed for a few moments. "I know all those files by heart, and I don't think Inspector Manley refers to him. But that's typical. Has Manley slipped up?"

"No. Sampson belongs to your end, Charlie, the London end. The whole case has switched to you now."

Vosper grinned. "It isn't my case, Temple, not unless I solve it. Who is Tony Sampson, how did he crop up?"

"He goes around with a girl from the club where Betty Stanway works, and he even seems to be acceptable to Tam Coley, the owner of the club. So there is a slight link with Desmond Blane through the Love-Inn."

Tite Street, of course, had gone down in the world since 1894, and the houses had been renumbered. Seven people appeared to live in the one building, and Tony Sampson had flat number seven. But he wasn't answering the bell that afternoon.

Charlie Vosper rang the other bells, and two or three voices answered through the grill. "I'm Jeremy," said Inspector

Vosper, and a buzzer sounded mysteriously behind the door. He pushed and it opened. Charlie Vosper grinned at his own guile.

A selection of mail on the table inside the hall revealed a letter to Tony Sampson, which confirmed that he wasn't in. But it was fourpenny post and had been posted the day before, so it wouldn't have been delivered first thing in the morning. Charlie Vosper shrugged. He was still in a devious mood.

"I think we have sufficient grounds for entering his flat," he murmured. "Reasonable suspicion."

They went through the lushly carpeted hall and up the stairs to the second floor. Several doors opened as they passed, anxious people waiting for Jeremy, and the doors closed again at the formidable sight of Inspector Vosper. Flat number seven was at the end of a brief corridor.

Paul watched as Vosper applied a device on his key ring to the safety lock, and almost at once the door swung open. It was a luxurious flat for somebody earning £1750 a year; it had the hushed atmosphere of expensive carpets, tapestry and furniture. There was a colour television, a hi-fi set with stereophonic speakers, and other expensive electronic toys were around the room. The colour television set had been left on, and a dazzling spectrum of colour flickered meaninglessly in search of a picture. The body of Tony Sampson lay on the sofa.

The kitchen was off the small entrance hall, a compact room in which even the onions were hung as decoration. This had been a man who preferred the best. He had the best of bedrooms beyond the sitting room, with a large bed and built-in wardrobes. The whole flat looked as if it had been designed by a stranger, and nothing of Tony Sampson except his conspicuous wealth came through.

"Don't touch anything," said Charlie Vosper.

It looked as though Tony Sampson had been watching television when his caller arrived. There was no sign of a struggle, and no sign of forced entry, so it must have been a friend of his who smashed open Tony's head. The murder weapon was the poker which lay in the fireplace. The sickly smell came from the newly splattered blood on the sofa.

Charlie Vosper picked up the telephone to call his men into action.

"I might as well be going," said Paul. "You'll obviously be tied up here for a while."

"Temple!" Inspector Vosper's tone had reverted to the brusqueness of a man on duty. "Where are you going?"

"I thought I might take the rest of the afternoon off," said Paul, "you know, wander into a West End club and relax for an hour. I find the sight of so much blood disturbing." Paul smiled apologetically. "And this is the second man I've found with his head battered in like this. I'll soon think I've become allergic to them."

"Keep away from the Love-Inn. I don't want you frightening off our man, whoever he might be. You only confuse things with all your theories about whizz kids and grammar school boys." The inspector laughed unfairly. "I knew this poor bloody kid couldn't be responsible for all that planning and organisation. Look at him. He's been killed by an old-fashioned gangster working in an old-fashioned way.

Paul nodded. "They've grown panicky."

Paul left flat number seven and closed the door behind him. In the corridor he paused to light a cigarette, and as he did so he realised he was being watched by the man from flat number five. A little man with bags under his eyes and a Vidal Sassoon haircut. He looked like a depraved adolescent, but on closer inspection he was probably forty-five and with it.

"You must be Jeremy," he said precisely. "Is something wrong in there?"

"The name is Temple. Why, did you hear something wrong?"

"I never hear anything, duckie, I was well brought up. And anyway, there's so much to hear in these flats it could become a full time occupation. I prefer to dabble in things." He smiled a dazzling white friendly smile. "I'm Butch Bendix, I model and things like that."

"Hello. Were you a friend of Tony Sampson?"

"Not intimately. I sometimes took in his milk and said hello on the stairs. Why the past tense? Is he dead? His hands fluttered nervously to his dyed grey temples. "Oh my God! That must have been what the noise was about. I heard him screaming."

"Can I come in?"

"Mm? Yes, of course. It's funny, you don't look like a Jeremy really."

"The name is Paul Temple."

Mr. Bendix's flat was identical to the one Paul had just left, except that he had different toys and there were flowers in vases everywhere and a window box in the living room had reduced the daylight to a green hue. He sat on a sofa with his legs curled under him and sighed.

"When did you hear him scream?" asked Paul.

"About an hour ago."

"So what did you do?"

"My dear Jeremy, what should I have done? I heard him scream, but of course I assumed he was probably having an extra good time. Would you have interfered?"

"The name is Paul Temple. I might have peered through the letter box."

Butch Bendix giggled. "I did that. But I frightened the wits out of myself. He was a big sulky looking man with black hair smarmed down with grease. A vicious looking fellow."

Paul picked up the evening paper from the coffee table and pointed to the photograph of Blane on the front page. But Bendix only said that might have been the man he saw, or it might be the Prime Minister, mightn't it?

"Did Mr. Sampson often scream in the middle of the day?"

Butch Bendix pouted. "No, he was such a dull young man, terribly conventional. He had a girlfriend who was all flesh and make-up. I stood in the lift with her once and the smell made me feel quite faint. So much scent that you wondered what she was trying to conceal. She looked like an all-in wrestler. I think her name was Gloria, which sounds like somebody with a lot of hair and a certain spirituality, don't you think?"

"Tony Sampson wasn't conventional," said Paul.

"He was something to do with banks." Butch Bendix grinned. "He said he provided inside information for bank robberies, which was a terribly sad thing to say. He was always trying to make himself sound interesting! He spent most of his day at home watching television and drinking from a grotesque cocktail cabinet. He had nothing else to do most of the time, and insufficient imagination to think anything up. Isn't that rather conventional?"

Paul told him to read what it said under Desmond Blane's photograph, and left the man to his studies.

"Gloria what did you say her name was?" Paul asked him at the door.

"What? I've no idea. But this man is wanted for robbing banks! She was a dancer, which Tony Sampson seemed to think was important. A girl who would never have made it as a shorthand typist. Just fancy, perhaps I *have* been living next door to a man who gave inside information for bank robberies. What fun!"

Tony Sampson the neighbour had simply been another of the bed-sit people who spent most of his time killing time, a rich little bloke who watched too much television. He had a few friends and drove a white Jaguar, dressed quite sharply and said good morning on the stairs. He had aspired to a level of financial acceptability, and having achieved it made no impression. Butch Bendix had wondered why he had bothered.

Paul had left his car in the car park at Scotland Yard. He decided to leave it there and go straight to the Love-Inn. At least it wouldn't be towed away from there. He nodded to the police driver on the pavement and went off in search of a taxi.

It was the rush hour and taxis were hard to come by; the streets were thronged with law abiding office workers scurrying to their law abiding homes in the peaceful suburbs. That was probably an illusion, but in the warm May sunshine they looked very harmless, and the dead bodies of bank clerks and bank robbers seemed highly exceptional. When the taxi pulled up outside the Love-Inn the place looked sadly uninteresting. Night and neon lights and football crowds were needed to provide the right atmosphere.

Paul went into the Love-Inn. It smelled of dust and plastic seat covers and yesterday's greasepaint. The auditorium was empty and the bar was shut. Paul glanced at his watch and found that it was six o'clock; the afternoon show was over and the evening show did not begin until seven thirty. And May was a slack month. Paul went off in search of Tam Coley or Gloria, or anybody. He found Tam in the office.

"Have a drink," said Tam.

Gloria Storm was the tall girl with the long brown hair who had slapped and tickled with Tony Sampson in the corridor. She shared the dressing room with Betty Stanway. She listened to Paul's account of his visit to Tony Sampson's flat with an aloof fatalism. Tam Coley was doing enough worrying for both of them.

"What with Betty leaving suddenly, and the police in the club every night asking questions," he complained, "the Love-Inn is becoming too hot. I'm disturbed."

Gloria was not surprised. "Tony Sampson was a prune," she said loftily. "He was always trying to impress someone, and now he's succeeded. That's what comes of trying for the big money." She spoke with the broken bottle accent of an expensive school. "I always told him that the only way to get rich was to have rich parents or a rich husband, but he wouldn't listen. He wanted to do it the hard way."

"I suppose that's understandable," Paul murmured.

"Why? He didn't want to do anything with the money, except not work, and perhaps have a string of dancers at his disposal. That doesn't do anybody any good: look what it's done to Tam Coley."

Coley grinned sheepishly at Paul.

"Was he rich?" Paul asked. "Until a month ago he earned less than two thousand pounds a year, and then he was fired."

"No, he wasn't rich. The white Jaguar he drove was second hand on the never-never. He only talked big. He claimed to be in with a team of bank robbers, but I expect that was only bluff. Said that he was their financial adviser. You know what these men are like. He thought he was a great lover, but as soon as he had his trousers down—"

"Mr. Temple doesn't want to hear about that," Tam Coley interrupted.

"How long had you known Tony Sampson?"

"About four months. He burst into the club with a shower of money, so of course Rita had to assign someone to him. That was me. I have a natural talent for helping men to spend more money than they can afford."

"I'm beginning to feel sorry for Tony Sampson."

She smiled radiantly. "He was up to his ears in debt within a few weeks, but it was all in a good cause. It made Tam Coley that much richer, didn't it, darling?"

"I always say that a few debts are a spur to a man," Coley said with an attempt at humour.

"It didn't worry him. Tony always put on a show." Paul wondered whether her arrogance came from being the daughter of a bishop or of an innate conviction that all men were fools. She took personal pleasure in the fact that she had exacerbated Tony Sampson's financial difficulties. "We threw a party on stage when he got the sack from the bank; it was terribly amusing. Tony got paralytically drunk."

Paul didn't need to know any more. He turned to Tam Coley. "Have you been in the club all day?"

"Hereabouts. Why?"

"Did Desmond Blane look in during the early afternoon?"

"I shouldn't think so—"

Gloria Storm interrupted. "He telephoned. He was asking for Betty, but she wasn't here. Rita told him we hadn't seen Betty since she gave in her notice."

Paul was about to hurry from the dressing room, but as an afterthought he turned back to Gloria. "I suppose you don't know where Betty might be, do you? I think she's in real danger."

"No. She was planning to go to Dublin, but something must have gone wrong. Des Blane sounded absolutely frantic." She laughed at the absurdity of other people's problems. "He said he would kill Betty when he got his hands on her!"

"He wasn't joking," said Paul as he turned and cannoned into Rita Fletcher. "Oh. I'm sorry."

"What's going on?" Rita asked. She took Paul's hand to restrain him. "Is Betty still intending to leave the country with Des?"

"Something like that," said Paul. "Have you any suggestions to make, before she ends up dead?"

"Only indirectly," she said with a wistful smile. "Why don't we have supper together?"

As they climbed into a taxi and moved off towards Leicester Square, Paul noticed a nervous Tam Coley standing in the club doorway watching them go. He obviously needed a drink.

CHAPTER 11

THEY went to Paul's favourite fish restaurant, and at that time of the evening it was not too crowded. They were able to sit at the corner table on the first floor. But Rita ate the food as if her mind were on something else, and Paul wondered whether they might just as well have gone to the fish and chip shop round the corner from the Love-Inn. Except that they wouldn't have had such a delicious Chablis, and Rita Fletcher was drinking that with a little more appreciation.

"I can understand your being concerned about Betty," he began remonstratively, "but you mustn't spoil good cooking—"

"I'm worried about the club." She looked with direct brown eyes at Paul for a moment. "I've put in eight years of my life to make Tam Coley a millionaire, and if the little runt has ruined it all—" She looked away. "I don't know what I'll do to him."

"How," Paul asked carefully, "do you know he's ruined it all?"

She was surprised. "The police have been there a dozen times and you were there again this evening. Don't tell me there's no connection between those bank robberies and the Love-Inn."

"Oh yes," Paul agreed. "There's a connection. How do you find the fish? Are you certain this isn't red mullet? It's so similar to the bass that I can't always tell." He ate a little more with approval. "What connection exactly did you have in mind?"

"Do you know who runs the gang?" she asked, with another direct stare.

"Yes, I think so. But for the moment I think it's more important to find Betty Stanway. She'll be dead before morning otherwise."

"Do you think so?" Her hand trembled a little as she finished the course. "Why would Desmond Blane kill her?"

"Because she is no further use to him, and she could now be dangerous to the person at the top. That was reason enough to kill Tony Sampson."

"Poor Tony." She lit a cigarette while the waiter brought them cheese and biscuits. "I wish Des had never come to the club. I knew there would be trouble sooner or later. I used to deal with him myself, because I thought Tam would lose his head."

"You mean when Des was running the protection racket?" Paul murmured.

"Yes." She smiled nervously. "You knew about that? He came to the club about five years ago. Or maybe it was six, I don't remember, and Tam refused to pay. Tam was a fool. He thought because we weren't in America the protection gangs couldn't do us any harm."

"What happened?" Paul asked.

"I paid protection. Tam was always plastered by nine o'clock, and so Des used to collect at half past nine on Fridays. I don't believe in being a hero. I carried on paying until last year when the outfit Des belonged to was broken up. What would you have done?"

Paul nodded non-committally. "I carry a few insurance policies."

"Most of the people Des worked with went to gaol. He came to the club asking for a job after that. We were quite good friends, but it was purely business. I told him we had all the bouncers we needed."

"You're suggesting he went to Tam after you turned him down?"

"Maybe." Rita looked weary as she sipped her brandy, cupping the glass in her warm hands and glancing at Paul across the rim. She shrugged her shoulders and smiled. "Maybe I don't care if Tam has ruined it all. I'm tired. I feel as if I've been running since I was seventeen, and where has it got me? Weary! I could do with a holiday." She looked her forty-two years. But Paul could not imagine the spirit in her accepting defeat for long.

"What would make a man like Tam Coley turn to crime?" Paul asked.

She laughed, and the life returned momentarily to her body. "What do you think the club business is in London? A church youth club with a better floor show? You have to be tough in this business, Mr. Temple, and you have to be tough to get up off the floor in New York and come to London with that kind of money. Tam isn't just a happy little lush."

"Is the club doing good business?"

"Of course it is. I run the place. I suppose I should have given him a bit more to occupy his mind, but I thought the girls and an unlimited supply of booze would keep him out of trouble." She sighed. "The girls will be thrown out of work as well, just when they were doing so well. Did you see them on television, or were you too busy fighting off that pompous politician?"

Paul agreed that they had been impressive.

Rita herself had started off as a dancer, and over another brandy she told Paul how she had learnt all she knew about the business.

"I was a good dancer," she said without humility. "But I knew that dancing wouldn't last forever. I moved over into management, and I've been very good at that. I've been so good at managing I've scared every man away, usually before he even got around to making a pass. So now it's me who is scared. It isn't easy to change jobs in middle age."

"I think you'll probably get by," Paul said sincerely. "A woman like you doesn't often fall on her face."

She looked amused and said she hoped so.

"Why don't you get your own club? Paul asked.

"I don't have Tam Coley's money."

"If Tam Coley went to gaol for master-minding these bank robberies, what would happen to the Love-Inn?"

She thought for a moment and then shook her head. "I doubt whether the Director of Public Prosecutions would give it to me for a birthday present. I suppose it would be sold."

Paul smiled sympathetically. "The D.P.P. is not very fair, is he? I think you've probably earned the club."

"It's my destiny to play second lead to people who have to be carried." She undid the top button of her ample corsage. "I'm feeling quite tipsy, for the first time in years. It's a shame, because I really quite enjoy it. Shall we have some Irish coffee?"

Paul ordered two Irish coffees.

"Do you hate self-pitying women?" she asked.

Paul shook his head sympathetically. "I think you've every reason to be fed up."

"You're nice, Paul Temple. Has anybody ever told you you're attractive? You don't have to work at being poised and charming, which is a change from the men one meets at the club. They're all so desperately trying to prove something that one forgets they aren't the whole of the masculine gender."

Paul tried not to be too suave with the waiter who was warming the brandy, pouring the coffee and making great play with the business of laying the cream on the top of the mixture. But the waiter seemed to expect an off-hand compliment.

"Has anybody ever told you that people who work in night

clubs have too many hang-ups?" Paul asked, deciding to put her on the defensive instead. "There's no difference between your customers and the ones who buy plastic flowers or mass produced greetings cards. What's so degrading about men who need a little impersonal sex?"

"I find our customers depressing. Take Tony Sampson, for instance, didn't you think he was depressing?"

"Of course. He was a sad little character, and you helped him to approximate his fantasy of himself. A lonely bank clerk who wanted to be a cut price playboy."

She said "And what's the harm in that, apart from the fact that he's dead? He was a sad little character, okay, but he was wildly in debt, and everybody soon knew it. He was just asking for somebody like Tam to put two and two together." She coughed and lit another cigarette. "Two and two. I hope I'm not too drunk to remember what that metaphor was. Yes, two was Desmond Blane the out of work gangster, and two was a bank clerk who knew about things. Four was a decent bank robbery." She grinned with pride in her addition. "I suppose you could say that Desmond Blane and Tony Sampson were destined for each other. It would have been perverse of Tam to have kept them apart."

Paul sipped his Irish coffee and felt warm. "My dear Rita, at this moment I don't care very much about Tam's guilt. I'm more worried about Betty Stanway. She is a nice girl and she is likely to be murdered. If you remember what you were like fifteen years ago, when you were worried about being a dancer for the rest of your life, you'll know why she got caught up in this. She's a girl like you were yourself."

"Poor Betty. I thought I was doing her such a favour when I fixed her up with Desmond Blane. I thought he had made good, was going straight. I suppose crooks never do really make good, do they?"

"Not often," Paul agreed.

"God knows where Betty is. She probably thinks that Desmond is a much maligned character in the first place, and that she can reform him in the second place. Women are strange creatures. I'm glad I'm not in her place, even though I'm drunk. Will you take me home?"

"Why?" asked Paul. "Have you told me what you were meaning to tell me? Because I knew all about the link between Desmond Blane the protection racketeer and Tony Sampson the man who needed Love."

She sighed and wrinkled her forehead. "I didn't intend to tell you anything you didn't know. That's not what conversation is all about. I wanted to talk to you, because I like you, and I wanted you to like me. I'm a successful woman, so I don't ask nonentities to hold my hand when I'm feeling depressed. Did you expect a revelation?"

"No," Paul admitted.

"So take me home, and we'll have a few more drinks. Unless you have somewhere more pressing to go. Make love to me, if you've had enough to drink. Anything, only please don't leave me alone tonight."

Paul waved to the waiter for their bill. He explained gently to Rita that she was a fine specimen of womanhood with lots of animal vitality, but that he was contentedly married. It sounded a little square, but he took her by the arm and hailed a taxi.

"Scotland Yard, please," he said to the driver.

Rita looked surprised. "Are you giving yourself up or running me in?" she asked ironically.

"I left my car there this afternoon."

She sat back in the taxi and made a conspicuous effort to stop feeling sorry for herself. She asked Paul about the things he had been doing these last few days. "The police must find you rather a strain," she said, "getting involved in their work."

"Charlie Vosper is an old friend of mine," he said, "and anyway it was Desmond Blane who involved me in this case. He killed a man in my garage."

"It's funny, he doesn't look like a killer."

"We can prove it this time," said Paul, "he was seen in Tony Sampson's flat at the time of the murder. So even if Arnold Cookson won't give evidence against his friend it won't matter."

"Who is Arnold Cookson?"

"You'd probably know him if you saw him," said Paul. "He visited the Love-Inn on New Year's Eve with Blane."

"I remember, he was an estate agent."

They pulled up outside Scotland Yard and paid off the taxi. Paul took Rita's arm again and went in search of his Rolls. She was slightly unsteady, but her mind was pursuing its main obsession with undiminished power.

"Of course," she said, "unless you find Desmond Blane you won't have enough evidence against Tam to arrest him, will you?"

"We won't have any evidence at all," Paul admitted.

She giggled as she climbed into the passenger seat of the Rolls. "In that case I hope you don't find him."

"What will you do if this business just fizzles out?" Paul asked her.

"I don't know. Maybe I'll persuade Tam to take me into partnership. I need a little security." She grinned with mischievous female guile. It wouldn't be blackmail to persuade him, her eyes seemed to indicate, because she had earned a place on the board.

"Where to?" Paul asked.

"I think I'll go back to the club."

CHAPTER 12

DESMOND BLANE wasn't behaving like a man eloping to a new life. He was jumpy. So the telephone had been out of order; what had he expected her to do? She had stayed put, so that at least he would know where to find her. As a child Betty had always been told by her mother to stay put whenever she was lost. Betty had stayed at the hotel.

"What the bloody hell are you doing here?"

"Des! I was so worried about you—"

"Are you packed?"

"Yes. I did ring, but they said the line was out of order—"

"Let's get going. You can pay the bill while I wait downstairs in the garage. Hurry up, for God's sake."

He gave her a fistful of notes and pushed her out of the lift at the ground floor. Des went down into the basement where the car park gave onto the Thames embankment. He was jumpy. Yet everything he had done so far had been cleverly worked out.

When the police are likely to be after you in force, he had told her, there's only one place to hide: in the best hotel in London. The law won't look for you there. And it had proved true, nobody had bothered her. Betty paid her bill and eventually located the car in the dark subterranean cavern.

Des was reading the evening paper by the courtesy light. "Jump in," he snapped.

She had done something wrong again. Des had been like

this when they had spent that last night together in Knightsbridge. And Betty remembered the three weeks of misery that had followed. She wished she knew what to say to him.

"What's the matter, Des?"

"We're in a hurry." He tossed the three suitcases and the holdall into the boot. "The police are onto us."

She sat beside him as they drove up into the embankment gardens; Des was concentrating, as if he didn't want to talk to her. Betty picked up the newspaper which he had been reading and tried to take her mind off her worries.

She had been looking forward to this for years. Ever since she had become a dancer. A nice rich husband and a nice remote rambling house. She knew exactly the kind of house she wanted, because she had seen a television programme about the west coast of Ireland and there were all of those farmhouses, next to castles and Martello towers and the sea stretching all the way to America. She had bought a big coffee table book which showed pictures of the rural life, with photographs of painters and poets who also lived there.

"Do you want lots of children, Des?"

"Do you mind? Keep an eye on the driving mirror in case we're being followed."

They were driving out through Hammersmith and onto the A4, being followed by several thousand cars and lorries. She wanted four children herself, all boys. Sturdy and independent little boys like Des, with his black hair and dark complexion. She wondered what the schools were like in Ireland.

"Will we be happy in Ireland, Des?"

He had been looking at a photograph of himself in the evening paper. That must have been what upset him. But the photograph didn't really resemble him. She smiled at the spiky looking man in the picture, and wondered whether he had looked like that ten years ago.

"Have you killed anyone?" she asked nervously.

"No, of course not. Will you stop asking stupid questions? I can't stand nagging women."

"I wasn't nagging, Des—"

"And don't argue!"

Of course he had robbed those banks, she knew that. When he had met her outside her parents' house that night Des had explained everything to her. He had been completely honest about it, and she had made him promise to give it up if he really wanted her to go away with him.

The plane left at half past eight from Heathrow. Betty noticed in the newspaper it had said that Des was thought to be planning to leave the country. Perhaps he was coming with her, instead of meeting her over in Dublin as they had arranged. But she didn't dare ask. They would soon be at Heathrow, and then she would know.

"Are we being followed?" he demanded.

Betty turned to look. A blue and white police car had just gone by on the other side of the motorway, but she couldn't tell whether it was chasing anybody. There were too many cars to tell. Des moved out into the fast lane and increased speed to something frightening.

Betty didn't care if they were killed. It would be better than going back to the Love-Inn, to Tam Coley and all those dirty old men, or to that grim little basement flat in Belsize Park. There was only one thing she really wanted, and that was to live with Des in the west of Ireland. And the police were trying to stop her.

Des wasn't like all those drooling men in the club. She remembered how they had made love in the caravan, after he had promised that his days of crime were over. That creepy Arnold Cookson had been asleep on the other side, and there were all those holiday makers on every side. She had been rather inhibited to begin with, but they had kept awake until four in the morning, talking and making love and talking, until Arnold Cookson woke up and complained. For the first time in goodness knows how long she had felt proud of herself.

"Paul Temple said you were using me," she said.

"When?"

"He came to see me yesterday at the club. It's all right, I didn't tell him anything. But you wouldn't use me, would you, Des?"

"As what?"

"I don't know. Do you really love me?"

"Of course I do," he said irritably. "I'm here, aren't I?"

"Yes."

They were still on the motorway and passing signs that indicated the turning off to Slough. Betty wondered when they would reach the airport. She got confused by all the M roads and A roads which never quite went to the same places. As far as she could remember Heathrow was on the A4.

"He seemed to think you were using me to get the money out of the country."

"Did you believe him?"

"No, Des, of course not."

Suddenly they were passing through Reading and she saw that they were turning off along the road to Oxford. They had left Heathrow a long way behind.

"Where are we going, Des?" she asked softly. "Aren't we going to Ireland?"

"We've had to change our plans, haven't we?"

"Oh, I see." She blew her nose and shrank into the seat. "I thought we were going to Ireland."

"We would have done if you hadn't talked to Mr. Paul bloody Temple!"

"I'm sorry."

She knew the way they were going, she remembered it from Saturday night when Des had picked her up outside the front door of her parents' house. But they didn't go to the caravan site this time. They took a different road round Banbury and went up a hill with trees on either side. At the top they turned left along a bumpy ridge.

Betty looked at the lights of Banbury spread out away in the distance and thought how beautiful it was. She supposed she ought to feel like a bride coming home. Perhaps they were going to live here for a while, until it was safe to go to Ireland. It looked remote enough. Des was still driving at an unnecessary sixty-five miles an hour, as if they were being followed.

Some gates flashed past and they were driving towards a large house which stood against the sky, black and gothic, perfectly remote from the police and all those people who wanted to spoil her chance of happiness.

As they drew up before the front door a small fox terrier ran out barking at the wheels of the car. Des tried to swerve the car at it, but they had stopped and the dog was unhurt.

"Des! You nearly killed—"

Her voice broke off as he took a Walther P.P.K. pistol from the glove compartment. He was aiming it at the dog when he saw a woman standing by the Hillman Imp at the side of the house. He pointed it at the woman instead.

Steve had been watching television by herself when she realised that Paul had missed the point. She should have been sketching out a few ideas for a series of book jackets, but that would have meant reading the books. She was watching television, wondering how to persuade Paul to read the books and tell her what they were about, when she saw on the news that Arnold Cookson had been arrested at the Red Trees Caravan Site.

The police wished to interview Desmond Blane and Betty Stanway. They had disappeared, and anybody who could provide information was asked to contact New Scotland Yard. Their two photographs were flashed briefly on the screen while it was explained that they might be making for Ireland.

Paul would be busily tracking them down, she thought, away for days in the cause of justice and Charlie Vosper. She would have to read the books herself. First novels by women; perhaps it wasn't necessary to read them; there would be the one about a girl at university having an abortion, the one about a girl hitting London and marrying a painter, the one about a sensitive young wife coping with children in N.W.1. Maybe the fourth book would combine all three plots. Steve smiled. It would be more interesting if the girl were abducted by a bank robber and kept a prisoner at . . .

I know where they are, she thought to herself.

Paul had missed the point when she had told him about Red Trees Farm. He had gone off with the police to the caravan site and they had made their arrest. But it was the farm itself which Cookson had sold to somebody in London.

"Come on, Jackson, we're going for a walk."

The dog was asleep under the television set. He growled at an imaginary Siamese cat, wagged his tail, and continued sleeping.

"Let's go for a car ride."

Jackson knew his way about, as usual, and he barked in recognition when they passed the caravan site. Steve was grateful for his company. He wouldn't be much protection in an emergency, but at least he would warn her if Blane was lurking about in the dark.

When they reached the top of the hill and parked beside the

farmhouse Steve began to have second thoughts about showing Paul how clever she was. Blane was a ruthless killer, and the reason everybody was so keen to find him was that he intended to kill again. Betty Stanway, Steve Temple, what was one more to him? Perhaps Steve had been rash.

The house appeared to be empty. There were no lights and she couldn't hear any movement. After waiting a few moments in case anybody had heard the car she stepped onto the gravel driveway. Jackson remained on the back seat.

"Coming?" she murmured. "They don't seem to have arrived yet."

He was probably afraid of the dark. Steve shrugged understandingly and went silently round to the back of the house. She noticed a barn twenty yards away, which might be useful if she had to hide. The farmhouse was probably eighteenth century; a few small latticed windows and thick stone walls; it had not been very well kept during the past few years. She noticed a broken window on the first floor, within easy reach of anybody who was standing on the back porch.

She kicked off her shoes and climbed onto the porch. Her stretch ski slacks would never be the same, but she got there and balanced precariously on the slate roof while she opened the window and slithered inside. She could feel her heart beating rapidly as she crossed the bathroom and went into a bedroom which occupied the front corner of the house. She hoped it was the exertion, but it might have been nerves. From that corner of the house she assumed she would see any car approaching the drive.

Steve made a rapid tour of the building, switching the light on and off instantaneously in each room, memorising the geography and learning what she could of the place. It was not lived in, but obviously somebody had been there recently because the kitchen was noticeably warm. Presumably a manager worked there during the day, responsible for the caravan site. He couldn't be responsible for the farm, because it wasn't farmed. Steve wondered whether there were laws to compel farmers to use their land, but she couldn't remember.

The telephone was in the hall. She rang the house in London, but Paul didn't answer. While she was wondering what to do next she heard Jackson barking outside. She dialled nine nine nine and asked for the police as she heard the car.

"Can you send out to Red Trees Farm immediately, please? I think Desmond Blane has just arrived."

She hurried to the side door and found that she was right. Desmond Blane was pointing a gun at her.

"Who are you?" he asked.

"Steve Temple. I've heard a lot about you. Hello, Betty. I've been expecting you." She smiled and held the door open for them. "I was about to make a pot of tea. You're probably thirsty after the journey."

"I'll do the organising," said Blane. He turned to Betty and asked, "Is this the woman who gave you a lift with Paul Temple on Saturday?"

Betty nodded.

"What are you doing here?"

Steve laughed. "I would have thought that was obvious. I came to prevent you from killing Betty. She didn't mean to become involved in your squalid little robberies, and I doubt even now whether she has the remotest idea what is going on."

Blane was hesitant. He ushered them into the kitchen and hunted through the cupboards for something to drink. He clearly didn't know his way around very well, but he had been there before. He found a bottle of whisky in the pantry.

"How do you mean to stop me killing Betty?" he asked.

Betty was so pale that by contrast with her auburn hair her

face looked almost sallow. She wasn't speaking. Bad as things were she probably knew they would get worse if she spoke, worse still if anybody acted.

"I called the police," said Steve. "They'll be here any moment."

He nodded. "I believe you." He raised the Walther again, pointed it at her heart and squeezed the trigger.

Steve heard the bang and heard the scream. For a second or so she wondered when she would die, and whether there would be any pain. Then she realised that Betty had grabbed Blane's arm. The shot had gone into the floor and Blane was using the gun as a club on Betty's head.

Steve threw herself across the room and wrestled for the gun. She wished she hadn't discarded her shoes. It was a doomed battle, two women and a playful dog were no match for Desmond Blane. She was hurled brutally to the stone floor and the impact stunned her.

"You beast," she muttered as somebody sat her up.

But the fight seemed to be over. Somebody else was holding the gun and Desmond Blane was running from the house. Then somebody said, "Darling, that's no way to speak to your husband. Are you all right?"

"Of course I'm all right," she gasped. "I just don't like dogs licking my ears."

"Des! Des, take me with you!"

Betty Stanway had a trickle of blood running down her face as she staggered to her feet. She was crying as she stumbled out of the doorway. The black Triumph 1300 was already moving when Betty pulled open the passenger door and fell into the car.

There was a roar from the engine, a hail of gravel from under the wheels, and the car shot away from the house towards the headlamps of a car coming towards it.

"Oh God," murmured Steve.

Desmond Blane drove straight at the on-coming car.

"Control to X Henry One. Proceed to Red Trees Farm immediately. Suspects Blane and Stanway thought to be in the vicinity. Take extreme caution, X Henry One, the suspect is dangerous and probably armed."

P.C. Bob Newby liked the bit about extreme caution. This was his own personal criminal and he intended to deal with him in his own special way.

"Can't you go any faster?" he said unpleasantly to P.C. Brooks.

Horace Brooks stepped on the accelerator and went through Banbury at seventy-three miles an hour. They took corners with the rear wheels slithering up onto the pavements, hit a gate on the narrow lane out of the town and sped on up the hill.

Bob Newby could hear the arrangements being made over the radio to send every available car out to the farm. It sounded as if nearly twenty cars would be joining them.

"Come on, for God's sake. I want to get there first."

Brooks smiled. "We'll get there first. I'm the best driver in the force."

They turned sharply left at the top of the ridge and hurtled along the bumpy lane. Bob Newby was on the radio telephone saying, "X Henry One to Control" when he realised that a car was driving straight at them.

"Pull over!" he shouted. "Christ—!"

Brooks stamped on the brakes and swung the wheel, they skidded towards the trees with the back of the car coming round to meet them as the oncoming car crashed into their side.

Betty screamed at the last moment, and threw herself against Desmond Blane's shoulder. She added to the impact as he was thrust against the steering column. The car buckled against the windscreen and showered her with fragments of glass. It seemed like minutes later that she pulled Des back from his position hunched over the wheel. He was obviously dead and blood was oozing across his chest.

The drive was instantly busy with policemen, running to the cars which had crashed and slamming doors, calling out instructions and running away again.

"She'll live," someone said inanely as he examined Betty.

They had hit the rear side of the police car as it was moving off the road, ramming it several feet into the woods and probably wrecking the engine. But the occupants of the car were unhurt. Betty watched helplessly as Paul Temple and Steve came over to her. Paul Temple prowled about, looked at Des, glanced at the back seat and then opened the boot.

"Hello, Betty," he said. "I'm sorry it has ended like this. We did try to avoid it."

"We were going away together, to Ireland," she said dully. "We were going to live in a big farmhouse."

"He was only using you," Steve said firmly. "He had intended to use you to get the money out of the country, and then he was going to kill you."

She shook her head. "I asked him about that, and he said he loved me."

Paul came round from the back of the car with Inspector Manley. It was the inspector who spoke. "Miss Stanway, is this your holdall?" When she shook her head he continued, "Do you know what it contains?"

"No. And I don't want to listen to all your lies about Des—"

Her voice trailed into silence when Inspector Manley opened the holdall. It was stuffed with bank notes.

"Come on," said Paul Temple, quietly, "we'd better take you home."

CHAPTER 13

"I don't think you would enjoy the Love-Inn," said Paul. "They don't really cater for women customers—"

"If you think you're going to enjoy it alone," said Steve, "you're wrong. I'm coming with you."

Paul shrugged in agreement and drove on past their house in Vincent Mews. It was early afternoon, so there wouldn't be any riotous football crowds in the club.

"We'll just pop in with Betty for a few minutes," he said, "and clear up the last few details of the case. It shouldn't take fifteen minutes." He drove slowly across Chester Square in case Steve should change her mind. "You could wait in the car—"

"I'll come with you."

Betty sat in the back seat as she had done on Saturday evening, only three days ago. It seemed longer. She was glumly silent, unappreciative of Steve's suggestion that she join a tennis club and meet a few nice insurance brokers and articled clerks. "It isn't so bad being a dull little housewife," Steve assured her.

"Des would have got away with it," she muttered, "if I hadn't hitched a lift from you."

"And at this precise moment you would have been stranded in Dublin." Paul spoke with what he hoped was brutal kindness. "If that telephone box hadn't been out of order you would have taken the plane by yourself and gone to Dublin with a hundred thousand pounds."

"Why is everybody so obsessed with money?" Betty asked wearily.

She had spent the night at Random Cottage and slept until eleven this morning. Her head no longer ached and the horror of Red Trees Farm was already becoming as remote as a nightmare. It was over, and she had to go on living in Belsize Park.

Betty watched Steve Temple with envy, because she had and took for granted all of the happily married things which Betty had wanted so much from Des. It wasn't only the home and enough money, it was the self assurance. Betty wondered how people could be so self assured. Even after they had nearly been killed Steve Temple had gone home and made them all cups of cocoa. She asked how Paul had known where to find them, as if it were unthinkable that he shouldn't have known.

"I knew because of something Rita Fletcher said," he had explained. "She said that Arnold Cookson was an estate agent. She wouldn't have known that he was an old con, and obviously when he went to the Love-Inn on New Year's Eve it must have been in his professional capacity. I wondered whether it was to sell a large piece of farmland."

"I thought you had missed the point—"

"I had. But when I came to think about it I realised that the robbers' using the caravan site couldn't be wholly coincidental. I realised that was what you had meant, and of course I panicked." Which seemed improbable, Betty thought resentfully. "I knew that you would be pottering about at the farm getting into a scrape. I don't think I've ever driven so fast in England."

They had laughed together and gone up to bed. Betty had stared at the stars for more than an hour in the clear night sky, and then the cocoa and the sleeping tablets had begun to work.

Betty hadn't wanted to go back to the Love-Inn, but what she wanted didn't seem very important. Steve Temple had arranged it all, and here they were.

Paul parked behind the Love-Inn, fed the meter, and walked through to the stage door. That way at least Steve missed the photographs of pink bosoms and ecstatic smiles, the ambiguous advertisements and the queue of men in shabby raincoats waiting to see somebody else's fantasies enacted.

Paul said good afternoon to the toothless old stage door keeper. "Is Mr. Coley about?" he asked. "We're returning one of his absconding girls."

"If you'd like to wait in the office, Mr. Temple," he said with a disconcerting three fingered salute. "I'll tell Mr. Coley you're here."

"Thanks. I've also arranged to meet Inspector Vosper—"

"No, he hasn't arrived. Are we being raided?"

They went into Rita Fletcher's office and waited. Steve wandered round examining the photographs on the walls while Paul tried to be reassuring to Betty. The brassy blare of the band close at hand indicated that the afternoon show was in progress, and eventually Steve went off to stand in the wings. Paul shrugged his shoulders. She was over twenty-one.

"When you see the inspector this time he'll want to know all about a bank clerk called Tony Sampson. He'll ask you—"

"Tony Sampson?" Betty repeated in surprise.

"Yes. Tell him the truth, Betty, tell him everything you know about Tony Sampson."

Betty was disbelieving. "I don't know anything about him."

"Are you sure?"

"Well, I know he's Gloria's boyfriend. But I've only spoken to him half a dozen times. I don't even like him." She considered for a moment. "Why should the inspector be interested in him?"

"Because he's dead," said Paul. "He was the inside tip-off for the bank robberies."

"You mean Des killed—?" But she broke off in confusion.

Rita Fletcher was standing in the doorway. "Hello, Betty," she said softly. "We've been worried about you." She put an arm round Betty's shoulders. "You'd better get changed, darling, you're on in fifteen minutes."

Betty nodded and went off to join the other girls.

Rita watched her go. "She'll be all right in a few days, Mr. Temple." She turned to him. "Well, I gather I have to congratulate you."

"Really?"

She smiled mockingly. "Don't you read the newspapers? They're giving you the credit for what happened at that farm yesterday evening. It all reads rather excitingly. They say that if it hadn't been for you the police wouldn't have caught up with Des Blane or retrieved the money."

Paul spread out his hands in modesty. "That's not strictly true. The police would have caught up with them, but it might have taken them slightly longer to catch up with everybody else, and the Love-Inn would have been a dancer short."

"I hope I wasn't too much of a bore last night," she said.

"You were charming company, and you were very helpful. I'm only sorry that your business career has to end like this."

"Like what?" The cold shrewdness which Paul had noticed several times last night was in her eyes again. "Des was killed, wasn't he? So you'll never have the evidence to convict Tam."

"Yes and no," said Paul. He offered his cigarette case. "Would you like a cigarette?"

She raised an eyebrow as she hesitated, then she took one.

"You'll hardly believe this," he continued, "but you've been very helpful on both occasions that I've met you."

"Me?" She lit her cigarette from the book of matches which Paul had produced. "I don't understand."

"You remember when you left me in Betty's dressing room? You were looking for her, and in fact she was out front with Mr. Coley?" He gave her the book of matches. "That was when I found these matches in the ashtray."

Rita stared at the matches. "Well?" she asked blankly.

"The Gateway Motel, Banbury," he indicated. "Not unnaturally I jumped to the conclusion that Betty had picked up the matches when she'd visited the motel. I assumed she had spent Saturday night there with Desmond Blane." He smiled apologetically. "I went to the motel and questioned the manager, and I was wrong. He had never seen Betty Stanway."

"Go on," Rita said flatly.

"Fortunately just as we were leaving, my wife Steve forgot her handbag. It was then that I realised what had happened."

Rita nodded. "They were my matches. Betty had taken them from my handbag."

"That's right," said Paul. *"I went back to the manager, and this time instead of describing Betty I described you. He knew you immediately."*

"Angus Lomax is pretty observant," she said. "I met Desmond there when it became too risky to meet here at the club." She stared at Paul for a moment as she stubbed out her cigarette, then she smiled. "Thank you for being so frank, Mr. Temple, although you could have mentioned this last night."

"I don't like eating alone. And I needed to find out where Blane had taken Betty. I knew you were only trying to keep me occupied so that they could escape. But you did so with great panache. Perhaps when you are a very old lady you'll be able to retire to Red Trees Farm. It will still be there."

She sighed. "I shouldn't have bought it. I was greedy. Who

needs a big farm like that?"

She began gathering together the oddments and personal belongings from the desk. She looked at the pictures on the wall and said what the hell? It was time to go.

"I'm glad you didn't arrest Tam," she said. "He would have been very upset." She laughed briefly. "All those things I told you about Tam, they were all true. Except that it was me."

"I know."

Suddenly the door to the office was thrown open by Tam Coley. He was looking wild and nervous. "Rita, where have you been? The police are here, swarming all over the place." He hurried over to the drinks cabinet, paused to look at his watch and turned severely away. "What the hell do they want?"

She smiled at him for a moment. "I rather think they want me, Tam."

Steve was standing in the wings watching The Melody Girls enacting a dance ritual called, plagiaristically, Desire Under the Elms. There was much frenzied removal of clothes as the girls combined death and fertility symbolism in their worship of trees.

"Betty is a good dancer," she murmured. "Very expressive." But she seemed more absorbed by the men in the audience. "It's the perspiration on their bald heads that is so fascinating," she continued. "Do you notice the way it catches the light?"

"Let's go," said Paul.

"I expected from the nervous way you tried to stop me from coming," Steve said regretfully, "that I might find the show more enjoyable. Why don't they—?"

"They probably didn't think of it."

Paul led her through the private door and out into the foyer where she laughed at the advertisements. Several solitary males looked round at her in alarm.

"By the way, the stage door keeper gave me a message for you," Steve said as she followed him into the street. "Brian Clay telephoned and wants you to ring him back at the television studio. Something about appearing on his programme to discuss the master minds of crime."

Paul perceptibly increased his pace, through the side street and back to the car. He glanced apprehensively at the loungers in case they should be reporters.

"We won't hang around in London," he said. "Let's go straight back to Broadway. We were going for a long weekend, or was it a month?"

Steve slipped contentedly into the Rolls. "I'm relieved," she said. "It's too much of a strain when you go on the box. You can put all that nervous tension into the novel about masterminds of crime."

Paul drove in silence for a while, then he answered, "I don't think I'll write that novel after all."

"Darling, don't be silly, it was a marvellous idea. I can already see that grammar school boy with his two A levels moving in on the traditional crime syndicates, he's a perfect character. I see him as somebody like Tony Sampson."

Paul nodded. "That's what is wrong with the idea. Tony Sampson was an unimaginative fool, and faced with people like Desmond Blane he was a dead duck. I was lucky to solve this case. Dammit, I ought to have known right at the beginning that Rita was behind it all."

"No, darling," Steve said soothingly, "you couldn't have. Don't blame yourself—"

"The coincidence of Desmond Blane picking up Betty after we dropped her at the end of her road! Obviously that wouldn't have been a coincidence. So who would have told Desmond Blane when and where to pick her up? It could only have been Rita!"

Steve nodded slowly and said no more.

Rita had combined high intelligence with an intuitive understanding of the people she was dealing with, but what had made her so redoubtable was a savage ruthlessness. Paul wondered as they left London behind whether ruthlessness wasn't still the principal characteristic of a successful criminal, as with a successful anything else.

"She seemed so successful already," said Steve, "with all those photographs on the wall of her office. Everybody seemed to love her. Even you weren't exactly unfriendly."

"I think she just wanted to play the lead," said Paul.

They sped on through the warm summer afternoon, along the Western Avenue and then right, on towards Oxford.

"Well," said Steve, "at least there'll be a welcome when we reach Random Cottage. Jackson will be pleased to see us."

FRANCIS DURBRIDGE

SEND FOR PAUL TEMPLE

After a series of robberies, Scotland Yard are mystified. In the latest a night watchman is attacked, and in his last breath manages to gasp out 'The Green Finger'. This is not the first time the phrase has come to the attention of the Yard; it was also said by a man who was wanted in connection with another robbery as he died from drowning. Who or what is the 'Green Finger'? The public are alarmed and the press demand that the Yard 'Send for Paul Temple!' Aided by a young, pretty, reporter known as Steve Trent, Paul is faced with solving a deepening and widening mystery.

THE GENEVA MYSTERY

Swinging between London and Geneva, Paul Temple and Steve are involved in a case that involves finding the answer to one vital question: is Carl Milbourne, who was thought to have perished in a car accident, still alive? A Hollywood film producer and a famous actress believe he is, but there are others who are determined to stop the Temples discovering the truth. There are deep mysteries to uncover and plenty of action and suspense which might even involve the death of Paul Temple, unless he can act quickly . . .

FRANCIS DURBRIDGE

PAUL TEMPLE INTERVENES

Sir Graham Forbes, of Scotland Yard, often needs Paul's help with his latest tricky case. Myron Harwood, an American, is found dead in a country lane. Further celebrity murders follow. A common factor is that a note is left with each victim on a small piece of cardboard. On it is the inscription: 'The Marquis'. A private investigator named Rita Cartwright who is investigating the murders also ends up as a victim. It is time for Paul Temple to intervene after requests from both Sir Graham Forbes, of Scotland Yard, and the Home Secretary. But what can he do?

PAUL TEMPLE & THE MARGO MYSTERY

Expensive Margo 'designer' coats; an industrialist; a pop star who is obviously frightened; and a psychiatrist with a very strange secretary all have something in common - they are somehow connected to a mysterious warning received from a fairground, and a terrifying case that Paul Temple and Steve have to solve.

FRANCIS DURBRIDGE

PAUL TEMPLE & THE CONRAD CASE

Betty, the daughter of Dr Conrad, disappears from her finishing school in Bavaria. Unable to solve the mystery, the police invite inveterate investigator Paul Temple to help trace the missing schoolgirl. The only clue to her whereabouts is a cocktail stick found in her bedroom. How on earth can Temple work from just that? The police have faith in him, but does he? All is revealed in yet another of Francis Durbridge's masterful mystery adventures.

Paul Temple & The Madison Case

Sam Portland is on board a luxury trans-Atlantic liner, as are Paul Temple and Steve. An innocent introduction involves the Temples in a case in which murder, blackmail and terror feature as the pace quickens, taking the story to an English mansion house, Amsterdam, and a houseboat on the River Thames. The secret is what happened to Sam Portland's lost years. But who is Madison?

3175391R00077

Printed in Great Britain
by Amazon.co.uk, Ltd.,
Marston Gate.